THE FIGURED WHEEL

By Robert Pinsky

POETRY

Sadness And Happiness (1975)

An Explanation of America (1979)

History of My Heart (1984)

The Want Bone (1990)

PROSE

Landor's Poetry (1968)

The Situation of Poetry (1977)

Poetry and the World (1988)

TRANSLATIONS

The Separate Notebooks,
by Czeslaw Milosz (1983)

The Inferno of Dante (1994)

THE FIGURED WHEEL

New and Collected Poems, 1966–1996

ROBERT PINSKY

THE NOONDAY PRESS

FARRAR, STRAUS AND GIROUX

NEW YORK

The Noonday Press
A division of Farrar, Straus and Giroux
19 Union Square West, New York 10003

Copyright © 1996 by Robert Pinsky
All rights reserved
Published simultaneously in Canada by HarperCollinsCanadaLtd
Printed in the United States of America
First published in 1996 by Farrar, Straus and Giroux
First Noonday paperback edition, 1997
Fifth printing, 1998

The Library of Congress has catalogued the hardcover edition as follows:
Pinsky, Robert.
    The figured wheel : new and collected poems, 1966–1996 / Robert
Pinsky. — 1st ed.
    p.   cm.
    Includes index.
    ISBN 0-374-15493-7
    I. Title.
PS3566.154F54   1996
811'.54—dc20   95–47617
                                                                          CIP

ACKNOWLEDGMENTS

Sadness And Happiness first published by Princeton University Press, 1975; *An Explanation of America* first published by Princeton University Press, 1979; *History of My Heart* first published by The Ecco Press, 1984; *The Want Bone* first published by The Ecco Press, 1990.

Grateful acknowledgment is made to the editors of the following periodicals where previously uncollected poems first appeared: "The City Dark," "Desecration of the Grave of Rose P.," and "Impossible to Tell" in *Threepenny Review*; "Ginza Samba" in *TriQuarterly*; "Poem with Refrains" and "The Heartmoss" in *Antaeus*; "Round," "The Tuning," "Creation According to Ovid," "The Ice Storm," and "If You Could Write One Great Poem, What Would You Want It to Be About?" in *The New Republic*; "In Berkeley" in *Ploughshares*; "The Day Dreamers," "Everywhere I Go, There I Am," "House Hour," "Street Music," "Soot," and "Falling Asleep" in *The New Yorker*; "Avenue" in *The Boston Phoenix*; "Homecoming" and "Love Crown" (Paul Celan) in *The Paris Review*; "Body" and "Spirit" (Boris Christov) in *Partisan Review*; "Song on Porcelain" (Czeslaw Milosz) in *The New Republic*; "Isaac Leybush Peretz" (Moshe Leib Halpern) in *Agni*; "The Rhyme of Reb Nachman" in *Wigwag*; "From *The Inferno of Dante*: Canto XXXIV" in *Agni*.

CONTENTS

HISTORY OF MY HEART (1984)

AN EXPLANATION OF AMERICA (1979)

NEW POEMS

THE CITY DARK

In the early winter dusk the broken city dark
Seeps from the tunnels. Up towers and in gusty alleys,

The mathematical veil of generation has lit its torches
To light the rooms of the mated and unmated: the two

Fated behind you and four behind them in the matrix
Widening into the past, eight, sixteen, thirty-two,

Many as the crystal dream cells illuminating the city.
Even for those who sleep in the street there are lights.

Like a heavy winter sleep the long flint cold of the past
Spreads over the glinting dream-blisters of the city, asleep

Or awake, as if the streets were an image of the channels
Of time, with sixty-four, one hundred and twenty-eight,

The ancestral net of thousands only a couple of centuries back,
With its migrations and fortunes and hungers like an image

Of the city where the star-dispelling lights have climbed
And multiplied over the tenements and outlying suburbs

Like a far past of multitudes behind us in the glistering web
Of strands crossing, thousands and tens of thousands

Of lives coupled with their gains, passions, misfortunes.
Somewhere in the tangled alleyways, a rape. Somewhere

A spirit diffused winglike, blind along the stretched wires
Branching the dark city air or bundled under the streets,

Coursing surely to some one face like an ancient song *Do re,
Re la sol sol.* Somewhere diaspora, somewhere recognition.

Back here one died of starvation, here one thrived. Descendant,
The bitter city work and the shimmering maternal burden

Of music uncoil outward on the avenues through smoky bars,
By televisions, beyond sleepers while the oblivion of generation

Radiates backward and then forward homeward to the one voice
Or face like an underground pool, through its delicate lightshaft

Moonlit, a cistern of light, echoing in a chamber cellared under
The dark of the city pavement, the faintly glittering slabs.

GINZA SAMBA

A monosyllabic European called Sax
Invents a horn, walla whirledy wah, a kind of twisted
Brazen clarinet, but with its column of vibrating
Air shaped not in a cylinder but in a cone
Widening ever outward and bawaah spouting
Infinitely upward through an upturned
Swollen golden bell rimmed
Like a gloxinia flowering
In Sax's Belgian imagination

And in the unfathomable matrix
Of mothers and fathers as a genius graven
Humming into the cells of the body
Or cupped in the resonating grail
Of memory changed and exchanged
As in the trading of brasses,
Pearls and ivory, calicos and slaves,
Laborers and girls, two

Cousins in a royal family
Of Niger known as the Birds or Hawks.
In Christendom one cousin's child
Becomes a "favorite negro" ennobled
By decree of the Czar and founds
A great family, a line of generals,
Dandies and courtiers including the poet
Pushkin, killed in a duel concerning
His wife's honor, while the other cousin sails

In the belly of a slaveship to the port
Of Baltimore where she is raped
And dies in childbirth, but the infant
Will marry a Seminole and in the next
Chorus of time their child fathers
A great Hawk or Bird, with many followers

Among them this great-grandchild of the Jewish
Manager of a Pushkin estate, blowing

His American breath out into the wiggly
Tune uncurling its triplets and sixteenths—the Ginza
Samba of breath and brass, the reed
Vibrating as a valve, the aether, the unimaginable
Wires and circuits of an ingenious box
Here in my room in this house built
A hundred years ago while I was elsewhere:

It is like falling in love, the atavistic
Imperative of some one
Voice or face—the skill, the copper filament,
The golden bellful of notes twirling through
Their invisible element from
Rio to Tokyo and back again gathering
Speed in the variations as they tunnel
The twin haunted labyrinths of stirrup
And anvil echoing here in the hearkening
Instrument of my skull.

POEM WITH REFRAINS

The opening scene. The yellow, coal-fed fog
Uncurling over the tainted city river,
A young girl rowing and her anxious father
Scavenging for corpses. Funeral meats. The clever
Abandoned orphan. The great athletic killer
Sulking in his tent. As though all stories began
With someone dying.

                When her mother died,
My mother refused to attend the funeral—
In fact, she sulked in her tent all through the year
Of the old lady's dying. I don't know why:
She said, because she loved her mother so much
She couldn't bear to see the way the doctors,
Or her father, or—someone—was letting her mother die.
"Follow your saint, follow with accents sweet;
Haste you, sad notes, fall at her flying feet."

She fogs things up, she scavenges the taint.
Possibly that's the reason I write these poems.

But they did speak: on the phone. Wept and argued,
So fiercely one or the other often cut off
A sentence by hanging up in rage—like lovers,
But all that year she never saw her face.

They lived on the same block, four doors apart.
"Absence my presence is; strangeness my grace;
With them that walk against me is my sun."

"Synagogue" is a word I never heard,
We called it *shul*, the Yiddish word for school.
Elms, terra-cotta, the ocean a few blocks east.
"Lay institution": she taught me we didn't think
God lived in it. The rabbi just a teacher.

But what about the hereditary priests,
Descendants of the Cohanes of the Temple,
Like Walter Holtz—I called him Uncle Walter,
When I was small. A big man with a face
Just like a boxer dog or a cartoon sergeant.
She told me whenever he helped a pretty woman
Try on a shoe in his store, he'd touch her calf
And ask her, "How does that feel?" I was too little
To get the point but pretended to understand.
"Desire, be steady; hope is your delight,
An orb wherein no creature can be sorry."

She didn't go to my bar mitzvah, either.
I can't say why: she was there, and then she wasn't.
I looked around before I mounted the steps
To chant that babble and the speech the rabbi wrote
And there she wasn't, and there was Uncle Walter
The Cohane frowning with his doggy face:
"She's missing her own son's *musaf*." Maybe she just
Doesn't like rituals. Afterwards, she had a reason
I don't remember. I wasn't upset: the truth
Is, I had decided to be the clever orphan
Some time before. By now, it's all a myth.
What is a myth but something that seems to happen
Always for the first time over and over again?
And ten years later, she missed my brother's, too.
I'm sorry: I think it was something about a hat.
"Hot sun, cool fire, tempered with sweet air,
Black shade, fair nurse, shadow my white hair;
Shine, sun; burn, fire; breathe, air, and ease me."

She sees the minister of the Nation of Islam
On television, though she's half-blind in one eye.
His bow tie is lime, his jacket crocodile green.
Vigorously he denounces the Jews who traded in slaves,
The Jews who run the newspapers and the banks.
"I see what this guy is mad about now," she says,
"It must have been some Jew that sold him the suit."
"And the same wind sang and the same wave whitened,
And or ever the garden's last petals were shed,
In the lips that had whispered, the eyes that had lightened."

But when they unveiled her mother's memorial stone,
Gathered at the graveside one year after the death,
According to custom, while we were standing around
About to begin the prayers, her car appeared.
It was a black car; the ground was deep in snow.
My mother got out and walked toward us, across
The field of gravestones capped with snow, her coat
Black as the car, and they waited to start the prayers
Until she arrived. I think she enjoyed the drama.
I can't remember if she prayed or not,
But that may be the way I'll remember her best:
Dark figure, awaited, attended, aware, apart.
"The present time upon time passëd striketh;
With Phoebus's wandering course the earth is graced.

The air still moves, and by its moving, cleareth;
The fire up ascends, and planets feedeth;
The water passeth on, and all lets weareth;
The earth stands still, yet change of changes breedeth."

ROUND

What was the need like driving rain
That struck the house and pelted the garden
So poorly planned? What was the creature
That needed to hide from the stunning torrent
Among the piers of the stone foundation
Under the house

That groaned in the wind? The seedlings floated
And spun in furrows that turned to runnels
Of muddy water while the hidden watched
Apart from the ones that lived inside.
The house was pounded and stung by the wind
That flailed the siding

And pried at the roof. Though the beams looked sound
The rooms all shook. Who were the ones
Shaken inside and the one that hid
Among the stones all through the storm
While the whole failed garden melted to ruin?
What was the need?

IN BERKELEY

Afternoon light like pollen.

This is my language, not the one I learned.

We hungry generations with our question
Of shapes and changes, Did you think we wanted
To be like you?

I flicker and for a second
I'm picking through rubbish
To salvage your half-eaten muffin, one hand
At my ear to finger a rill of scab.

Not native
To California, with olive and silver
Leaves like dusty sickles flashing
In the wind, the eucalyptus bend
And whisper it to the hillsides, Did you think
We wanted to be like you?
The tall flourishers, not what they were.

I sniff one and lift my leg and leave
A signature of piss.

Or the feathery stalks of fennel
Burgeoning in the fissured pavement crazed
And canted by the Hayward Fault.
Outside the mosque or commune they grow chin-high,
Ghostly, smelling of anise
In the profligate sun—
Volunteers, escapees, not what they were.

A tile-domed minaret clad in cedar shingle
Grafted at a corner of the shingle house.
A Sufi mother and child come out, the boy

In mufti, shuffling his sneakers through the duff,
Holding her hand.

Mother.

Her cotton tunic and leggings are white,
And from the tapering pleated cylinder
Of her white vertical headdress
To the shoes white like nurse's shoes
Except for her hands and pink face
She is a graceful series of white tubes
Like an animated sheet. I wonder if
They shave their heads. Did you think we
Wanted to be like you?

Sister. Once maybe a Debbie or June,
A Jewish sophomore
From Sacramento or a cornsilk daughter
From Fresno or Modesto.

She puts me in the carseat, she fastens my belt.

Conversion. The shaven, the shriven, the circumcised,
The circumscribed—her great-grandmother
Bleeding a chicken, in her matron's wig
Not what she was.
And Malcolm's brother
Telling him in visiting hours *Don't eat pork*
So that he sat down Saul, and got up Paul.

The demonstrator
At the Campanile in her passion
Shouting at a white-haired professor
As he passed, *Old man—why don't you die?*

Forgive me little mother that I will savor
The flesh of pigs. We have forgotten
The Torah and the Koran, on every
Work day and holy day alike
We take up harvesting knives and we sweat
Gathering the herbs of transformation. This
Is my language, not the one I learned.

CITY ELEGIES

I. The Day Dreamers

All day all over the city every person
Wanders a different city, sealed intact
And haunted as the abandoned subway stations
Under the city. Where is my alley doorway?

Stone gable, brick escarpment, cliffs of crystal.
Where is my terraced street above the harbor,
Café and hidden workshop, house of love?
Webbed vault, tiled blackness. Where is my park, the path

Through conifers, my iron bench, a shiver
Of ivy and margin birch above the traffic?
A voice. *There is a mountain and a wood
Between us—* one wrote, lovesick—*Where the late*

Hunter and the bird have seen us. Aimless at dusk,
Heart muttering like any derelict,
Or working all morning, violent with will,
Where is my garland of lights? My silver rail?

II. "Everywhere I Go, There I Am"

Hot days of errands and badges, paper, shrill rage
Of sparrows morning and evening. At sunset
A clearing stroll around the square and down
A steep street twisting to the edge of the narrows,

The brick embankment path and the iron rail
The same as always. The water. All through your body
A steady twinkling of ceasing and being, the cells
That die by millions and replicate themselves

So every seven years your substance is new,
But the same score, the same scar making a faint
Crescent along your temple, always fading,
The blood all different but the same from day

To day, the city birds along the harbor
Working the cracks and hedges, the titan moan
Of a tanker blasting and receding, the range
Of noises a fretwork of the bay, the night.

III. House Hour

Now the pale honey of a kitchen light
Burns at an upstairs window, the sash a cross.
Milky daylight moon,
Sky scored by phone lines. Houses in rows
Patient as cows.

Dormers and gables of an immigrant street
In a small city, the wind-worn afternoon
Shading into night.

Hundreds of times before
I have felt it in some district
Of shingle and downspout at just this hour.
The renter walking home from the bus
Carrying a crisp bag. Maybe a store
Visible at the corner, neon at dusk.
Macaroni mist fogging the glass.

Unwilled, seductive as music, brief
As dusk itself, the forgotten mirror
Brushed for dozens of years
By the same gray light, the same shadows
Of soffit and beam end, a reef
Of old snow glowing along the walk.

If I am hollow, or if I am heavy with longing, the same:
The ponderous houses of siding,
Fir framing, horsehair plaster, fired bricks
In a certain light, changing nothing, but touching
Those separate hours of the past
And now at this one time
Of day touching this one, last spokes
Of light silvering the attic dust.

IV. Street Music

Sweet Babylon, headphones. Song bones.
At a slate stairway's base, alone and unready,
Not far from the taxis and bars
Around the old stone station,
In the bronze, ordinary afternoon light—
To find yourself back behind that real
City and inside this other city
Where you slept in the street.
Your bare feet, gray tunic of a child,
Coarse sugar of memory.

Salt Nineveh of barrows and stalls,
The barber with his copper bowl,
Beggars and grain-sellers,
The alley of writers of letters
In different dialects, stands
Of the ear-cleaner, tailor,
Spicer. Reign of Asur-Banipal.
Hemp woman, whore merchant,
Hand porter, errand boy,
Child sold from a doorway.

Candy Memphis of exile and hungers.
Honey kalends and drays,
Syrup-sellers and sicknesses,
Runes, donkeys, yams, tunes
On the mouth-harp, shuffles
And rags. Healer, dealer, drunkard.
Fresh water, sewage—wherever
You died in the market sometimes
Your soul flows a-hunting buried
Cakes here in the city.

V. Soot

Archaic, the trains mated with our human blood.
Stone trestle, abutment wall. Above the tracks
A rakish exile Santa lashed to a pole.
Black cinders, burdock, sumac, Pepsi, cellophane,
Each syllable a filament in the cord
Of a word-net knotted in the passionate shadows
Of skeletal vine and beanpole in one back yard
Along the embankment. Here with dirty thunder
Deliberate heavy creatures before the light
Of morning made the bedroom windows tremble
With lordly music, and their exhalations
Tingled our nostrils. Railbed tavern and church
Of former slaves, synagogue of the low,
Sicilian grocery, Polish crèche. A seed
Of particles that Zeuslike penetrated
The bread and carboned the garden tomatoes—even
Our sheets that bucked and capered in the wind
Flashed whiter than others, tempered by iron black
Bleaching to armor in silver winter sun.

VI. *The Tuning*

Soon in this plaza high above the harbor
Under the statue of St. Magnus Martyr
The gypsy orchestra will begin to play.

Down on the borders of the immigrant ghetto
Couples are gathering at the Montenegro
And the Club République, but at the close of day

These strings of lights and early summer weather
Bring us here: smell of traffic, tentative laughter
From café tables, a trickle of television

Leaking from the open window of an apartment
Above us. Clean cotton, perfume, garlic, the sunset
Making the pavement red with expectation:

And now we are the city—the mighty avenues
Named for historic dates, the alleyways,
The brands of car and liquor, the souk, the stone

Obelisk in the old slave market. Now the nervous
Tangle of tones and scales is suspended, the players
All schooling their single root to the raised baton.

AVENUE

They stack bright pyramids of goods and gather
Mop-helves in sidewalk barrels. They keen, they boogie.
Paints, fruits, clean bolts of cottons and synthetics,
Clarity and plumage of October skies.

Way of the costermonger's wooden barrow
And also the secular marble cinquefoil and lancet
Of the great store. They persist. The jobber tells
The teller in the bank and she retells

Whatever it is to the shopper and the shopper
Mentions it to the retailer by the way.
They mutter and stumble, derelict. They write
These theys I write. Scant storefront pushbroom Jesus

Of Haitian hardware—they travel in shadows, they flog
Sephardic softgoods. They strain. Mid-hustle they faint
And shrivel. Or snoring on grates they rise to thrive.
Bonemen and pumpkins of All Saints. Kol Nidre,

Blunt shovel of atonement, a blade of song
From the terra-cotta temple: Lord, forgive us
Our promises, we chant. Or we churn our wino
Syllables and stares on the Avenue. We, they—

Jack. Mrs. Whisenant from the bakery. Sam Lee.
This is the way, its pavement crackwork burnished
With plantain. In strollers they bawl and claw. They flourish.
Furniture, Florist, Pets. My mongrel tongue

Of *nudnik* and *criminentlies*, the tarnished flute
And brogue of quidnuncs in the bars, in Casey's
Black amber air of spent Hiram Walker, attuned.
Sweet ash of White Owl. Ten High. They touch. Eyes blurred

Stricken with passion as in a Persian lyric
They flower and stroke. They couple. From the Korean,
Staples and greens. From the Christian Lebanese,
Home electronics. Why is that Friday "Good"?

Why "Day of Atonement" for release from vows?
Because we tried us, to be at one, because
We say as one we traffic, we dice, we stare.
Some they remember that won't remember them—

Their headlights found me stoned, like a bundled sack
Lying in the Avenue, late. They didn't speak
My language. For them, a small adventure. They hefted
Me over the curb and bore me to an entry

Out of the way. Illuminated footwear
On both sides. How I stank. Dead drunk. They left me
Breathing in my bower between the Halloween
Brogans and pumps on crystal pedestals.

But I was dead to the world. The midnight city
In autumn. Day of attainment, tall saints
Who saved me. My taints, day of anointment. Oil
Of rose and almond in the haircutting parlor,

Motor oil swirling rainbows in gutter water.
Ritually unattainted, the congregation
File from the place of worship and resume
The rumbling drum and hautbois of conversation,

Speech of the granary, of the cloven lanes
Of traffic, of salvaged silver. Not shriven and yet
Not rent, they stride the Avenue, banter, barter.
Capering, on fire, they cleave to the riven hub.

THE ICE-STORM

IN MEMORY OF BERNIE FIELDS

Dear Robert, Thank you for trying to rig
A conduit for me—linkage, blank, bandage, this
Contraption made of grammar, with "I" for "he":

•

Words are no clumsier than what we use to trace
Tangled-up branches on the family tree
Of some culprit virus stowed in its rootclot.

•

Voice not you nor I, I not what I was or am,
You not what you are or were—poker crony,
Acquaintance, seeking what germ strewn in the sodcloud?

•

Flailing for instructive failure. *"That's life,"*
Muttered—not an adage and not an answer
To *What is life?* (Not my field, though nearly.)

•

What is a life?: that is the better question,
As I'd have said even before the cancer
Churned me across dark water to this other side:

•

No opalescent temple, no sages fringed and sidelocked,
No smoking field where a hero craves a cottage.
No void no terraces no planisphere. Nothing you know.

•

The day that Leslie read those poems to me
He wasn't sure I was listening, dark shape
Unspeaking swollen on the pillows. Tell him I was.

•

What is a life? A specimen, or a kind?
A savage craving or civil obituary
Architecture of birth, attachment, achievement?—

·

The *Times* rehearsing with mediated, Roman
Sweetness the names of my dear kin, so cherished
In the molten hold of attachment, sweet cooling lava;

·

Or honey of ink aggrandizing, gratifying
(" . . . one of the great virologists of the century"),
Meaning: a success, like everybody else.

·

When you hear the *Yisgadal v'yiskadash sh'may rabah*
When the beloved one hurling her handful of earth
Staggers at the brink as if buffeted by wind

·

When the congregation responds *Y'hay sh-may*
Rabah m'varah, l'olam ul-ol-may ol maya—it's
Now my mouth is the flared bell of a silver horn

·

Now my eyes lidded by the wings of a dragonfly look
Inward for billions of miles, Now my feet are two
Crystals that leave no prints. O the poker game!

·

Closed system, boyish ritual first Sunday evening
Of the month, more innocent than boyish, none smoking, few
Cursing, never more than a second beer, game, lightness.

·

Wanting deeply to win, and that wanting what we play
To laugh at, stakes high enough to terrify our
Selves at fourteen, low enough to parody that fear.

·

My brain a clay vessel my fingers unlit candles
My lights a cello, cabalistic rhythms of Spade
Heart Club Diamond royalty in Gypsy embroidery.

·

Permission, remission, the Washington AIDS job
My doctors said was too great a risk for me. Now
My heart is fluted amber, umbrage of texts, When

·

Thou cut down thy harvest in the field, and hast forgot
A sheaf in the field, thou shalt not go again to
Fetch it, for it will be for the stranger,

·

The fatherless and the widow, Remember thou
Lived a bondsman in the land of Egypt. *Yisgadal
V'yiskadash* trembling life, crystal or viral,

·

Lifespan of the ice-storm the week after I died
That lasted for three days: separate lucid twigs
Still coated with chrism each morning, gutters

·

Still filigreed with leaf-ice, diamonded branches
Bowed heavy with light, at dusk still rosy,
Mysterious light melted to a sheen by morning

DESECRATION OF THE GRAVESTONE
OF ROSE P. (1897–1924)

(Antiphony with "Church Monuments" by George Herbert)

A cautionless flagon threw the heart unphrased,
The devil's tongue. We thought ourselves evil, and
To prove it in our own eyes we four striplings
Ventured long off to the boneyard October night.

Drives all at last with lights, brews, hammers, crowbars,
Long-handled shovel. Exhalation, male
Exhilaration, primates packing out
Under clear autumn Zodiac with dead

To desecrate. Dry cells, sixpacks, work gloves,
Rocking a headstone downright unison chanting,
Sad granite bromides rocking in a widening socket,
Earthsmelling, smooth. Appliance of iron crow

Into the space, team cursels and gigging, shoves,
Shovelblade under a graven toppling. These laugh
At jet and marble put for signs, To sever
The good fellowship of dust, And spoil the meeting.

And what shall point out them, When they shall bow,
And kneel, and fall down flat To kiss those heaps,
Which now they have in trust? A coffin dragonworm
Incaution through the packing. Devlin's bung.

Farts of demons. Cold sweat, cold beers, a fatal must.
Cackles and whispers and the pissing-on
Of headstone soilbeds. Spatter and mist of pisses
And badder yet, the striking of oval portraits,

Photographs from the nineteenteens and so on
Well sealed in domes of thick defiant glass
Banged with a hammer. Glancing off cheekbone and gaze,
Cracked glaze, glance clouding white time's bleach. Crazed glass,

That when thou shalt grow fat And wanton in
Thy cravings, thou mayst know, That flesh is but
The glass, which holds the dust That measures all
Our time; which also shall Be crumbled into

Dust, prancing like Shiva, glancing off cheekbone, one stone
Barked trunklike, with truncated limbs stiff symbolizing
A life cut off too early, set in the awful
Stone bark in her calm oval an oval faced

Young woman, dark, How free from lust, Dear Flesh,
Eaten by Kali, smashed by Shiva, partially
Effaced, deathfashion. Harsh breath panted in dispassion,
Drunk flagging. Unchristian, Sir. Joosh moluments,

Flame's phlegmshaped characters. Take a letter: Dear Flesh,
That when thou shalt grow fat And wanton in
Thy cravings, thou mayst know. Flesh: Dung-de-*dung-dung*!
If the dung-carrier labors all a life long

In enlightenment and the priest or poet labors
In error, the dung-carrier attains a higher level
And returns at a higher level. Therefore I gladly
Trust my body to this school. In Gad we trust.

A hearthworn potion, contrition thrust between
The stirrup and the cup. A heartshorn passage,
How free from lust these ashes: Comparing earth
With earth in dusty heraldry and lines.

CREATION ACCORDING TO OVID

In the beginning was order, a uniform
Contending: hot cold, dry wet, light dark
Evenly distributed. The only sound

A celestial humming, void of changes
(*Playing the changes*, jazz musicians say).
And then the warring elements churned forth

The mother-father Shiva or Jehovah,
The dancing god who took a hammer and smashed
The atoms apart in rage and disarranged them

Into a sun and moon, stars and elements,
Ocean and land, the vegetation and creatures—
Including even Ovid playing the changes

In his melodious verses, including even
God the creator: himself divided male
And herself female by the sundering hammer

Held prancing, one foot on earth, one lifted in air.
From heaven to earth god came to visit the bodies
Of mortals, making himself a bull, an avid

Shower, a gibbon, a lotus. And to the one
Who had his child inside her, he promised to come
In any form she named. "Come to me naked,"

She said, "as in heaven with your sister-wife."
God wept, because he knew her human frame
Could not sustain that radiance, but he danced

For her and became an annihilating burst
Of light that broke her. God grieved, and from her body
He took the embryo and tearing his thigh

Sewed it up into the wound, and nine months later
Delivered the merry god whose attributes
His many titles embody: *Drunkard*; *Goat*;

The Twice Born—from the mother, then the father;
The Horned—because his father was a bull-god;
Sacrificed who dies and rises, and also *Slayer*;

The Orgiast and *The Tragedy Lord*; *The Liar*;
Breaker of Palace Walls; *The Singer* (all listed
In *Metamorphoses*, which Ovid burned

In manuscript because it was unfinished
When he was exiled, though other copies survived);
Disrupter, Smiler, Shouter in the Night.

THE HEARTMOSS

The creature was limber once. It came to grief
When it came browsing across the little puff

Of heartmoss and ate: sage furry cluster of spears
Tasting of anise and sourgrass, the little spores

Ingested whole in the sweetish dust of pollen.
Foreign, alive, unseen. Unfurled now, swollen

Into a sack that presses against the ribs
And squeezes the organs aside, the heartmoss bobs

Heavily, urging itself around the throes
Of the still-laboring heart. A displaced mass

Of veins and arteries coats the invading cyst
So that the growth is patterned like the moist

Stone of a halved fruit, or a brain. Stalled, quelled,
With cloudy eyes the creature stirs its bulk

Enough to ease the fibrous growth that floats
Pulling and shifting inside it, and navigates

Painfully by that sloshing internal compass,
Stumbling among the bodies of its fellows

Who move aside while gazing, ruminant,
At the great stumbler: ginger, ponderous, germinant.

FALLING ASLEEP

Black thatch, black root:
The unplowable prairie of night,
A matted snarl, the anchor tangle
Underbedding the restless grasses

Twisting on taproot and stem.
The train without horn or whistle
At the far perimeter fading
Perpetually closer or farther.

Now at the Registry of Lies
The brass cages are unlighted.
Even at the furious millworks
The belts and spindles are nearly

Stilled, only a few syllables
Flailing, heavy deceleration
Of the flywheel turning on its shaft
Steadily till it fails, dreamless.

Not dying, but the old figure
Of the body of the state,
The ruler the Head and his ministers
The Eyes the Ears the busy Tongue,

His soldiers the Feet, the Fingers
And Hands peasants and workers—
All stunned by a charm. Asunder.
From field and palace dark

Tendrils stream coiling to a nest
Of yielding branches
Cradling the crystal hoop, his Lights
His Heart his Genitals his Brain.

WAKING UP

But what woke just now at fifty-two years in narrow
Dormitory bed, clock on a chair, underpulse
Air-conditioning, damp tangle of dream plumage

Its afterbirth nimbus—night thong and mandible?
Possibly for a few seconds not more professor or
Poet or parent or writing conference pooh-bah

Than animal emigrant from those featherlands—the screen
Of boxes, the alleyway weeping, the black iceberg,
The garden deception, the fuck, the floating

Manhattan. Or naked, possibly for a second this vivid
Green moth smaller than a numeral, distinct, animula,
Alert visionless trembler, blundering in the light.

IF YOU COULD WRITE ONE GREAT POEM, WHAT WOULD YOU WANT IT TO BE ABOUT?

(Asked of four student poets at the Illinois Schools for the Deaf and Visually Impaired)

Fire: because it is quick, and can destroy.
Music: place where anger has its place.
Romantic Love—the cold or stupid ask why.
Sign: that it is a language, full of grace,

That it is visible, invisible, dark and clear,
That it is loud and noiseless and is contained
Inside a body and explodes in air
Out of a body to conquer from the mind.

INCANTATION

(Czeslaw Milosz)

Human reason is beautiful and invincible.
No bars, no barbed wire, no pulping of books,
No sentence of banishment can prevail against it.
It establishes the universal ideas in language,
And guides our hand so we write Truth and Justice
With capital letters, lie and oppression with small.
It puts what should be above things as they are,
It is an enemy of despair and a friend of hope.
It does not know Jew from Greek or slave from master,
Giving us the estate of the world to manage.
It saves austere and transparent phrases
From the filthy discord of tortured words.
It says that everything is new under the sun,
Opens the congealed fist of the past.
Beautiful and very young are Philo-Sophia
And Poetry, her ally in the service of the good.
As late as yesterday Nature celebrated their birth,
The news was brought to the mountains by a unicorn and an echo,
Their friendship will be glorious, their time has no limit,
Their enemies have delivered themselves to destruction.

IMPOSSIBLE TO TELL

TO ROBERT HASS AND IN MEMORY OF ELLIOT GILBERT

Slow dulcimer, gavotte and bow, in autumn,
Bashō and his friends go out to view the moon;
In summer, gasoline rainbow in the gutter,

The secret courtesy that courses like ichor
Through the old form of the rude, full-scale joke,
Impossible to tell in writing. *"Bashō"*

He named himself, "Banana Tree": banana
After the plant some grateful students gave him,
Maybe in appreciation of his guidance

Threading a long night through the rules and channels
Of their collaborative linking-poem
Scored in their teacher's heart: live, rigid, fluid

Like passages etched in a microscopic circuit.
Elliot had in his memory so many jokes
They seemed to breed like microbes in a culture

Inside his brain, one so much making another
It was impossible to tell them all:
In the court-culture of jokes, a top banana.

Imagine a court of one: the queen a young mother,
Unhappy, alone all day with her firstborn child
And her new baby in a squalid apartment

Of too few rooms, a different race from her neighbors.
She tells the child she's going to kill herself.
She broods, she rages. Hoping to distract her,

The child cuts capers, he sings, he does imitations
Of different people in the building, he jokes,
He feels if he keeps her alive until the father

Gets home from work, they'll be okay till morning.
It's laughter *versus* the bedroom and the pills.
What is he in his efforts but a courtier?

Impossible to tell his whole delusion.
In the first months when I had moved back East
From California and had to leave a message

On Bob's machine, I used to make a habit
Of telling the tape a joke; and part-way through,
I would pretend that I forgot the punchline,

Or make believe that I was interrupted—
As though he'd be so eager to hear the end
He'd have to call me back. The joke was Elliot's,

More often than not. The doctors made the blunder
That killed him some time later that same year.
One day when I got home I found a message

On my machine from Bob. He had a story
About two rabbis, one of them tall, one short,
One day while walking along the street together

They see the corpse of a Chinese man before them,
And Bob said, sorry, he forgot the rest.
Of course he thought that his joke was a dummy,

Impossible to tell—a dead-end challenge.
But here it is, as Elliot told it to me:
The dead man's widow came to the rabbis weeping,

Begging them, if they could, to resurrect him.
Shocked, the tall rabbi said absolutely not.
But the short rabbi told her to bring the body

Into the study house, and ordered the shutters
Closed so the room was night-dark. Then he prayed
Over the body, chanting a secret blessing

Out of Kabala. "Arise and breathe," he shouted;
But nothing happened. The body lay still. So then
The little rabbi called for hundreds of candles

And danced around the body, chanting and praying
In Hebrew, then Yiddish, then Aramaic. He prayed
In Turkish and Egyptian and Old Galician

For nearly three hours, leaping about the coffin
In the candlelight so that his tiny black shoes
Seemed not to touch the floor. With one last prayer

Sobbed in the Spanish of before the Inquisition
He stopped, exhausted, and looked in the dead man's face.
Panting, he raised both arms in a mystic gesture

And said, "Arise and breathe!" And still the body
Lay as before. Impossible to tell
In words how Elliot's eyebrows flailed and snorted

Like shaggy mammoths as—the Chinese widow
Granting permission—the little rabbi sang
The blessing for performing a circumcision

And removed the dead man's foreskin, chanting blessings
In Finnish and Swahili, and bathed the corpse
From head to foot, and with a final prayer

In Babylonian, gasping with exhaustion,
He seized the dead man's head and kissed the lips
And dropped it again and leaping back commanded,

"Arise and breathe!" The corpse lay still as ever.
At this, as when Bashō's disciples wind
Along the curving spine that links the *renga*

Across the different voices, each one adding
A transformation according to the rules
Of stasis and repetition, all in order

And yet impossible to tell beforehand,
Elliot changes for the punchline: the wee
Rabbi, still panting, like a startled boxer,

Looks at the dead one, then up at all those watching,
A kind of Mel Brooks gesture: "Hoo boy!" he says,
"Now that's what I call *really dead*." O mortal

Powers and princes of earth, and you immortal
Lords of the underground and afterlife,
Jehovah, Raa, Bol-Morah, Hecate, Pluto,

What has a brilliant, living soul to do with
Your harps and fires and boats, your bric-a-brac
And troughs of smoking blood? Provincial stinkers,

Our languages don't touch you, you're like that mother
Whose small child entertained her to beg her life.
Possibly he grew up to be the tall rabbi,

The one who washed his hands of all those capers
Right at the outset. Or maybe he became
The author of these lines, a one-man *renga*

The one for whom it seems to be impossible
To tell a story straight. It was a routine
Procedure. When it was finished the physicians

Told Sandra and the kids it had succeeded,
But Elliot wouldn't wake up for maybe an hour,
They should go eat. The two of them loved to bicker

In a way that on his side went back to Yiddish,
On Sandra's to some Sicilian dialect.
He used to scold her endlessly for smoking.

When she got back from dinner with their children
The doctors had to tell them about the mistake.
Oh swirling petals, falling leaves! The movement

Of linking *renga* coursing from moment to moment
Is meaning, Bob says in his Haiku book.
Oh swirling petals, all living things are contingent,

Falling leaves, and transient, and they suffer.
But the Universal is the goal of jokes,
Especially certain ethnic jokes, which taper

Down through the swirling funnel of tongues and gestures
Toward their preposterous Ithaca. There's one
A journalist told me. He heard it while a hero

Of the South African freedom movement was speaking
To elderly Jews. The speaker's own right arm
Had been blown off by right-wing letter-bombers.

He told his listeners they had to cast their ballots
For the ANC—a group the old Jews feared
As "in with the Arabs." But they started weeping

As the old one-armed fighter told them their country
Needed them to vote for what was right, their vote
Could make a country their children could return to

From London and Chicago. The moved old people
Applauded wildly, and the speaker's friend
Whispered to the journalist, "It's the Belgian Army

Joke come to life." I wish that I could tell it
To Elliot. In the Belgian Army, the feud
Between the Flemings and Walloons grew vicious,

So out of hand the army could barely function.
Finally one commander assembled his men
In one great room, to deal with things directly.

They stood before him at attention. "All Flemings,"
He ordered, "to the left wall." Half the men
Clustered to the left. "Now all Walloons," he ordered,

"Move to the right." An equal number crowded
Against the right wall. Only one man remained
At attention in the middle: "What are you, soldier?"

Saluting, the man said, "Sir, I am a Belgian."
"Why, that's astonishing, Corporal—what's your name?"
Saluting again, "Rabinowitz," he answered:

A joke that seems at first to be a story
About the Jews. But as the *renga* describes
Religious meaning by moving in drifting petals

And brittle leaves that touch and die and suffer
The changing winds that riffle the gutter swirl,
So in the joke, just under the raucous music

Of Fleming, Jew, Walloon, a courtly allegiance
Moves to the dulcimer, gavotte and bow,
Over the banana tree the moon in autumn—

Allegiance to a state impossible to tell.

THE WANT BONE

(1990)

FROM THE CHILDHOOD OF JESUS

One Saturday morning he went to the river to play.
He modeled twelve sparrows out of the river clay

And scooped a clear pond, with a dam of twigs and mud.
Around the pond he set the birds he had made,

Evenly as the hours. Jesus was five. He smiled,
As a child would who had made a little world

Of clear still water and clay beside a river.
But a certain Jew came by, a friend of his father,

And he scolded the child and ran at once to Joseph,
Saying, "Come see how your child has profaned the Sabbath,

Making images at the river on the Day of Rest."
So Joseph came to the place and took his wrist

And told him, "Child, you have offended the Word."
Then Jesus freed the hand that Joseph held

And clapped his hands and shouted to the birds
To go away. They raised their beaks at his words

And breathed and stirred their feathers and flew away.
The people were frightened. Meanwhile, another boy,

The son of Annas the scribe, had idly taken
A branch of driftwood and leaning against it had broken

The dam and muddied the little pond and scattered
The twigs and stones. Then Jesus was angry and shouted,

"Unrighteous, impious, ignorant, what did the water
Do to harm you? Now you are going to wither

The way a tree does, you shall bear no fruit
And no leaves, you shall wither down to the root."

At once, the boy was all withered. His parents moaned,
The Jews gasped, Jesus began to leave, then turned

And prophesied, his child's face wet with tears:
"Twelve times twelve times twelve thousands of years

Before these heavens and this earth were made,
The Creator set a jewel in the throne of God

With Hell on the left and Heaven to the right,
The Sanctuary in front, and behind, an endless night

Endlessly fleeing a Torah written in flame.
And on that jewel in the throne, God wrote my name."

Then Jesus left and went into Joseph's house.
The family of the withered one also left the place,

Carrying him home. The Sabbath was nearly over.
By dusk, the Jews were all gone from the river.

Small creatures came from the undergrowth to drink
And foraged in the shadows along the bank.

Alone in his cot in Joseph's house, the Son
Of Man was crying himself to sleep. The moon

Rose higher, the Jews put out their lights and slept,
And all was calm and as it had been, except

In the agitated household of the scribe Annas,
And high in the dark, where unknown even to Jesus

The twelve new sparrows flew aimlessly through the night,
Not blinking or resting, as if never to alight.

MEMOIR

The iron cape of the Law, the gray
Thumb of the Word:
Careless of the mere spirit, careless
Of the body, ardent
Elders of the passion of the soiled, the charred.

Snuffboxes, smells of Europe.
Mr. Sokol crooning blessings
Absently to himself,
Neither the words nor the music,
Nothing of the mind and nothing
Of the senses but only
That one thing that shall come to pass
If you will hearken diligently with all
Your heart and all your soul and lay up these,

My words, inside your heart and in your soul
And bind them as a sign upon your hand
And they will be as frontlets between your eyes:
So we wrote the words on squares of lambskin.

And we sealed them in wooden boxes bound
In leather and threaded the boxes
On black leather thongs and bound the thongs
With the sealed words in appointed places
Around our heads and arms.
It was like saying: I am this, and not that.

And you shall teach these words
To your children, boxes
Bound at the heart and the eyes,
And you shall speak of them when you sit
Inside your houses and when you stand

Speaking in the marketplace, and bound
In your heart entirely when you walk the avenues
And when you go to bed
And when you arise.

Tin canisters of money, tumblers
Of memorial wax.
Necktie of Poland, shirt of grief. Chickpeas
And Seagram's whiskey, blessings of mousefur lapels.
That, and not this.

And you shall fasten
These words onto your doorposts and your gates
And so we did, in boxes
Put for a sign and a memorial
To you upon your hands and at your eyes
And in your hearts and in your houses and so we wrapped
The thongs and boxes with words inside them
Around our hands and arms and heads
And wore them as frontlets between the eyes
Through the shadows of summer
With so many turns of leather
Around the fingers of the hand
Nearest the heart.
And when your son
Comes to you saying *what is this*
You shall tell him of the slaying
Of the firstborn of man and of beast
In Egypt when my father came out of Egypt.

Alien as a blue carapace and a trident.
Unreadable
Totems, gilt fringes, varnished books. A horse chestnut
Throwing its massive summer shade
Over the pavement.

But ye that did cleave
Unto the Lord your God are alive,
Every one of you, this day.
Smells of wool and chickpeas,
The sandstone building converted now

To a Puerto Rican Baptist church,
Clerestory and minaret.
A few blocks away, an immense blue
Pagan, an ocean, muttering, swollen:
That, and not this.

WINDOW

Our building floated heavily through the cold
On shifts of steam the raging coal-fed furnace
Forced from the boiler's hull. In showers of spark
The trolleys flashed careening under our cornice.
My mother Mary Beamish who came from Cork
Held me to see the snowfall out the window—
Windhold she sometimes said, as if in Irish
It held wind out, or showed us that wind was old.
Wind-hole in Anglo-Saxon: faces like brick,
They worshipped Eastre's rabbit, and mistletoe
That was Thor's jissom where thunder struck the oak.
We took their language in our mouth and chewed
(Some of the consonants drove us nearly crazy
Because we were Chinese—or was that just the food
My father brought from our restaurant downstairs?)
In the fells, by the falls, the Old Ghetto or New Jersey,
Little Havana or Little Russia—I forget,
Because the baby wasn't me, the way
These words are not. Whoever she was teaching to talk,
Snow she said, *Snow*, and you opened your small brown fist
And closed it and opened again to hold the reflection
Of torches and faces inside the window glass
And through it, a cold black sheen of shapes and fires
Shaking, kitchen lights, flakes that crissed and crossed
Other lights in lush diagonals, the snowcharmed traffic
Surging and pausing—red, green, white, the motion
Of motes and torches that at her word you reached
Out for, where you were, it was you, that bright confusion.

THE HEARTS

The legendary muscle that wants and grieves,
The organ of attachment, the pump of thrills
And troubles, clinging in stubborn colonies

Like pulpy shore-life battened on a jetty.
Slashed by the little deaths of sleep and pleasure,
They swell in the nurturing spasms of the waves,

Sucking to cling; and even in death itself—
Baked, frozen—they shrink to grip the granite harder.
"Rid yourself of attachments and aversions"—

But in her father's orchard, already, he says
He'd like to be her bird, and she says: Sweet, yes,
Yet I should kill thee with much cherishing,

Showing that she knows already—as Art Pepper,
That first time he takes heroin, already knows
That he will go to prison, and that he'll suffer

And knows he needs to have it, or die; and the one
Who makes the General lose the world for love
Lets him say, *Would I had never seen her,* but Oh!

Says Enobarbus, Then you would have missed
A wonderful piece of work, which left unseen
Would bring less glory to your travels. Among

The creatures in the rock-torn surf, a wave
Of agitation, a gasp. A scholar quips,
Shakespeare was almost certainly homosexual,

Bisexual, or heterosexual, the sonnets
Provide no evidence on the matter. He writes
Romeo an extravagant speech on tears,

In the Italian manner, his teardrops cover
His chamber window, says the boy, he calls them crystals,
Inanely, and sings them to Juliet with his heart:

The almost certainly invented heart
Which Buddha denounces, in its endless changes
Forever jumping and moving, like an ape.

Over the poor beast's head the crystal fountain
Crashes illusions, the cold salt spume of pain
And meaningless distinction, as Buddha says,

But here in the crystal shower mouths are open
To sing, it is Lee Andrews and The Hearts
In 1957, singing *I sit in my room*

Looking out at the rain, My tear drops are
Like crystals, they cover my windowpane, the turns
Of these illusions we make become their glory:

To Buddha every distinct thing is illusion
And becoming is destruction, but still we sing
In the shower. I do. In the beginning God drenched

The Emptiness with images: the potter
Crosslegged at his wheel in Benares market
Making mud cups, another cup each second

Tapering up between his fingers, one more
To sell the tea-seller at a penny a dozen,
And tea a penny a cup. The customers smash

The empties, and waves of traffic grind the shards
To mud for new cups, in turn; and I keep one here
Next to me: holding it awhile from out of the cloud

Of dust that rises from the shattered pieces,
The risen dust alive with fire, then settled
And soaked and whirling again on the wheel that turns

And looks on the world as on another cloud,
On everything the heart can grasp and throw away
As a passing cloud, with even Enlightenment

Itself another image, another cloud
To break and churn a salt foam over the heart
Like an anemone that sucks at clouds and makes

Itself with clouds and sings in clouds and covers
Its windowpane with clouds that blur and melt,
Until one clings and holds—as once in the Temple

In the time before the Temple was destroyed
A young priest saw the seraphim of the Lord:
Each had six wings, with two they covered their faces,

With two they covered their legs and feet, with two
They darted and hovered like dragonflies or perched
Like griffins in the shadows near the ceiling—

These are the visions, too barbarous for heaven
And too preposterous for belief on earth,
God sends to taunt his prophet with the truth

No one can see, that leads to who knows where.
A seraph took a live coal from the altar
And seared the prophet's lips, and so he spoke.

As the record ends, a coda in retard:
The Hearts in a shifting velvety *ah*, and *ah*
Prolonged again, and again as Lee Andrews

Reaches *ah* high for *I have to gain Faith, Hope*
And Charity, God only knows the girl
Who will love me—Oh! if we only could

Start over again! Then The Hearts chant the chords
Again a final time, *ah* and the record turns
Through all the music, and on into silence again.

THE WANT BONE

The tongue of the waves tolled in the earth's bell.
Blue rippled and soaked in the fire of blue.
The dried mouthbones of a shark in the hot swale
Gaped on nothing but sand on either side.

The bone tasted of nothing and smelled of nothing,
A scalded toothless harp, uncrushed, unstrung.
The joined arcs made the shape of birth and craving
And the welded-open shape kept mouthing O.

Ossified cords held the corners together
In groined spirals pleated like a summer dress.
But where was the limber grin, the gash of pleasure?
Infinitesimal mouths bore it away,

The beach scrubbed and etched and pickled it clean.
But O I love you it sings, my little my country
My food my parent my child I want you my own
My flower my fin my life my lightness my O.

SHIVA AND PARVATI
HIDING IN THE RAIN

Language of invasion, cloth of grief.
"How can I turn this wheel
that turns my life?"

Plural, playful.
Coat of morning-glory petals, bracelet
Of summer shadows,

The double-budded god
Having their fill
Of themselves. She

Cupped in his lap
Both wrapped in one cloak
Her arm clasping his neck.

Supplicants come, torturers
And sufferers on the wheel
Soldiers and scholars

Artisans and lovers, with words,
Dungeon and fashion, passion
And onion, from Venice ghetto,

From Prague dollar, stitches
Of captivity, inherited
Eyecolor or ear for music

Of raper and raped. Also this,
Also that, coupled the pair
Barely listen, turning

To embrace beyond reason—
Each is also the other, in touching
Touched, also the threads

Of rain and also the wheel
Of the sky also the foliage
So delicate only the torn-off

Wings of the green woodbeetle
Could represent it in a picture:
The rosecolored mother-father

Flushed, full, penetrated and
Also penetrated, entering
And entering, endowing

And also devouring, necklace
Of skulls and also ecstasy
Of hiding in raindrops, in

The storm, their eight sleek
Limbs and numberless
Faces all spokes from one trunk.

THE UNCREATION

The crowd at the ballpark sing, the cantor sings
Kol Nidre, and the equipment in our cars
Fills them with singing voices while we drive.

When the warlord hears his enemy is dead,
He sings his praises. The old men sang a song
And we protesters sang a song against them,

Like teams of children in a singing game;
And at the great convention all they did
They punctuated with a song: our breath

Which is an element and so a quarter
Of all creation, heated and thrown out
With all the body's force to shake our ears.

Everything said has its little secret song,
Strained higher and lower as talking we sing all day,
The sentences turned and tinted by the body:

A tune of certain pitch for questions, a tune
For *that was not a question*, a tune for *was it*,
The little tunes of begging, of coolness, of scolding.

The Mudheads dance in their adobe masks
From house to house, and sing at each the misdeeds
Of the small children inside. And we must take you,

They sing, Now we must take you, Now we must take
You back to the house of Mud. But then the parents
With presents for the Mudheads in their arms

Come singing each child's name, and buy them back:
Forgive him, give her back, we'll give you presents.
And the prancing Mudheads take the bribes, and sing.

I make a feeble song up while I work,
And sometimes even machines may chant or jingle
Some lyrical accident that takes its place

In the great excess of song that coats the world.
But after the flood the bland Immortals will come
As holy tourists to our sunken world,

To slide like sunbeams down shimmering layers of blue:
Artemis, Gog, Priapus, Jehovah and Baal,
With faces calmer than when we gave them names,

Walking our underwater streets where bones
And houses bloom fantastic spurts of coral,
Until they find our books. The pages softened

To a dense immobile pulp between the covers
Will rise at their touch in swelling plumes like smoke,
With a faint black gas of ink among the swirls,

And the golden beings shaping their mouths like bells
Will impel their breath against the weight of ocean
To sing us into the cold regard of water.

A girl sang dancing once, and shook her hair.
A young man fasting to have a powerful dream
Sang as he cut his body, to please a spirit.

But the Gods will sing entirely, the towering spumes
Dissolving around their faces will be the incense
Of their old anonymity restored

In a choral blast audible in the clouds,
An immense vibration that presses the very fish,
So through her mighty grin the whale will sing

To keep from bursting, and the tingling krill
Will sing in her jaws, the whole cold salty world
Humming oblation to what our mouths once made.

LAMENT FOR THE MAKERS

What if I told you the truth? What if I could?
The nuptial trek of the bower apes in May:
At night in the mountain meadow their clucking cries,

The reeking sulphur springs called Smoking Water,
Their skimpy ramparts of branches, pebbles and vines—
So slightly better than life, that snarl of weeds,

The small-town bank by comparison is Rome,
With its four-faced bronze clock that chimes the hours,
The six great pillars surmounted by a frieze

Of Cronus eating his children—or trying to,
But one child bests him because we crave to live,
And if that too means dying then to die

Like Arthur when ladies take him in his barge
Across the misty water: better than life,
Or better than truly dying. In the movies

Smoking and driving are better, a city walk.
Grit on the sidewalk after a thaw, mild air.
I took the steps along the old stone trestle

Above the station, to the part of town
I never knew, old houses flush to the street
Curving uphill. Patches of ice in the shade.

What if I found an enormous secret there
And told you? We would still feel something next
Or even at the same time. Just as now. In Brooklyn,

Among the diamond cutters at their benches
Under high Palladian windows full of a storm,
One wearing headphones listens to the Talmud.

What if he happens to feel some saw or maxim
Inwardly? Then the young girl in her helmet,
An allegorical figure called The Present,

Would mime for us the action of coming to life:
A crease of shadow across her face, a cross,
And through the window, washing stumps of brick,

Exuberant streaks and flashes—literal lightning
Spilling out into a cheery violent rain.
Worship is tautological, with its Blessed

Art thou O Lord who consecrates the Sabbath
Unto us that we may praise it in thy name
Who blesses us with this thy holy day

That we may hallow it unto thy holy blessings. . . .
And then the sudden curt command or truth:
God told him, Thou shalt cut thy foreskin off.

Then Abraham was better than life. The monster
Is better when he startles us. Hurt is vivid,
Sincerity visible in the self-inflicted wound.

Paws bleeding from their terrible climb, they weave
Garlands of mountain creeper for their bed.
The circle of desire, that aches to play

Or sings to hear the song passing. We sense
How much we might yet make things change, renewed
As when the lovers rise from their bed of play

And dress for supper and from a lewd embrace
Undress again. Weeds mottle the fissured pavement
Of the playground in a net of tufted lines

As sunset drenches a cinematic honey
Over the stucco terraces, copper and blue,
And the lone player cocks wrist and ball behind

His ear and studies the rusty rim again.
The half-ruined city around him throbs and glows
With pangs of allure that flash like the names of bars

Along San Pablo Avenue: Tee Tee's Lounge,
The Mallard Club, Quick's Little Alaska, Ruthie's,
Chiquita's, and inside the sweet still air

Of tobacco, malt and lime, and in some music
But in others only voices or even quiet,
And the player's arm pauses and pumps again.

PICTURE

Three men on scaffolding scatter cornflakes down
For people to see in black-and-white as snow,
Falling around the actor under the lights.

The actor hunches in the flakes, the set
Is a bitter street, the camera dollies in
And the monster stamps and sorrows, now he's lost,

He shakes his arms and howls, an ugly baby,
Nostrils forced open by little makeup springs.
The dust of cornflakes, trampled underfoot,

Infiltrates his lungs, he starts to wheeze
And so they take a break and start again.
Weeks later, he dies of pneumonia, maybe by chance—

But the picture is finished, people see the scene
And if they know, they feel the extra pathos,
Even if they joke a little about it. The movie

Is silent, cornflakes are a kind of health food,
It's all that long ago, although the picture
Survives as flecks of light and dark on substances

Not invented when they made it—or a play
Of information, a magnetic mist
Of charges, particles too fine to see.

ICICLES

A brilliant beard of ice
Hangs from the edge of the roof
Harsh and heavy as glass.
The spikes a child breaks off

Taste of wool and the sun.
In the house, some straw for a bed,
Circled by a little train,
Is the tiny image of God.

The sky is a fiery blue,
And a fiery morning light
Burns on the fresh deep snow:
Not one track in the street.

Just as the carols tell
Everything is calm and bright:
The town lying still
Frozen silver and white.

Is only one child awake,
Breaking the crystal chimes?—
Knocking them down with a stick,
Leaving the broken stems.

VISIONS OF DANIEL

Magician, appointed officer
Of the crown. He thrived, he never
Seemed to get older.

Golden curly head.
Smooth skin, unreadable tawny eyes,
Former favorite, they said,
Of the chief eunuch of Nebuchadnezzar,
Who taught him the Chaldean language and courtly ways
And gave him his name of a courtier:
"Daniel who was called Belteshazzar"
In silk and Egyptian linen.
Proprietor, seer.

The Jews disliked him,
He smelled of pagan incense and char.
Pious gossips in the souk
Said he was unclean,
He had smeared his body with thick
Yellowish sperm of lion
Before he went into the den,
The odor and color
Were indelible, he would reek
Of beast forever.

Wheat-color. Faint smell as of smoke.
The Kings of Babylon feared him
For generations.

And Daniel who was called in Chaldean
Belteshazzar, meaning spared-by-the-lion
Said as for thee O King I took
Thy thoughts into my mind
As I lay upon my bed: You saw O King a great
Image with His head of gold His heart

And arms of silver His belly and thighs of brass
His legs of iron His feet
Part of iron and part of clay
And then alas
O Nebuchadnezzar the image fell

And clay and iron
And brass and gold and silver
Lay shattered like chaff on the
Threshingfloor in summer.

Terrified Nebuchadnezzar
Went on all fours, driven
To eat grass like the oxen.
His body wet by the dews of heaven,
Hair matted like feathers, fingers
Hooked like the claw of the raven.

Interpreter, survivor,
Still youthful years later
When Nebuchadnezzar's son Belshazzar
Saw a bodiless hand
Scrawl meaningless words on the plaster
Mene Tekel Upharsin,
Interpreted by Daniel, You are finished,
God has weighed you and found you
Wanting, your power will be given
To the Medes and the Persians.

And both King Darius the Mede
And King Cyrus the Persian
Feared him and honored him.

Yellow smoking head,
High royal administrator.
Unanointed. He declined
To bow to images.

Then one night God sent him a vision
Of the world's entire future
Couched in images: The lion
With the wings of an eagle
And feet of a man, the bear

With the mouth in its side
That said, Devour Much Flesh,
The four-headed leopard
Of dominion, and lastly
The beast with iron teeth
That devoured and broke
And stamped and spat
Fiery streams before him.

And he wrote, I the Jew Daniel
Saw the horn of the fourth beast
Grow eyes and a mouth and the horn
Made war with the saints and
Prevailed against them.

Also, he saw a man clothed in linen
Who stood upon the waters
And said, As to the abomination
And the trial and the making white
Go thy way O Daniel, for the words
Are closed up and sealed till the end.

For three weeks after this night vision
I Daniel, he wrote, ate no pleasant
Bread nor wine, my comeliness
Turned to corruption, I retained
No strength, my own countenance
Changed in me. But I kept the
Matter in my heart, I was mute
And set my face toward the earth.
And afterward I rose up
And did the king's business.

Appalled initiate. Intimate of power.
Scorner of golden images, governor.
In the drinking places they said
He had wished himself unborn,
That he had no navel.

So tawny Belteshazzar or Daniel
With his unclean smell of lion
And his night visions,
Who took the thoughts of the king

Into his mind O Jews, prospered
In the reign of Nebuchadnezzar
And of his son Belshazzar
And in the reign of Darius
And the reign of Cyrus the Persian.

PILGRIMAGE

Near the peak. A clear morning,
Camphorous air of eucalyptus and mountain laurel
Lining the steep trail.

They chant in chorus as they climb,
Some of them in turns bearing
The ark—its hammered silver
Ornaments jangling, the pressure
Of polished cedar beams heavily
Afloat on their shoulders,
The others reaching in
To touch it as they dance and kiss
Their fingers that brushed it.

At the last of the dusty switchbacks
The trail grows wider and flatter
And they pause, flushed and shuffling.
They lower the ark to the earth,
A priest singing his aria
From beside it: Now I call you by your
True name—and they come forward:

One by one he fits
Embroidered blinders over their eyes
And guiding them singly by the hand
Singing the secret name of each
He leads them from the ark upward
To the cliff's edge, till the whole choir
Stands dancing in place
At the precipice, each man and woman
Chanting in a darkness.

At the prayer's end
They lift the blinders
To see the falls across the sheer vacancy:

Mountain light, the bridal veil
Skimming the great vertical
Rockface without interval,
Unquenchable granite in its plumage
Of air and falling water:
                    O Presence
You have searched me and seen me from afar,
My downsitting and my uprising.
Now nothing is next or before, there is
Nothing yet to enter, you have beset me
Behind and before, you have put
Your hand upon me, though I am
Fearfully and wonderfully made,
You have known me from afar.

Now for many of them
The falls appear motionless: hung
From the foamless brim in a vision
Of suspended flowing, falling
But unfallen. Through tears
Of pleasure they squint upward.

Now when they take the thick wizened scroll
Out from the ark in its white armor
And unfurl it, the crowned letters
Scorched and stained into the skin
In a catalogue of secret names—
                    Akhman, Ruveyne,
Yeosif, each sound indicated by characters
That form another sound, never to be uttered,
And behind each unutterable name
The name of that name's
Name in infinite regress—

They read themselves into the unchangeable
Book of the journey begun before
Your body was called up
And before it was made,
Before you were a seed packed in honey, before you

Fell from the brim, fashioned and torn
From the cold water that tumbles
Endlessly down the face of the mountain.

JESUS AND ISOLT

In the palace of Heaven God's holy angels were touching and fondling one another, gently and mutually, just as St. Augustine says they do, and laving their hair with oil of myrrh. But the Lord Jesus watched them with a scowl.

He said to his Mother, who sat on her throne of pearl, "Divinity is a leash to me, I miss the unquenchable days of living and dying, my old quarrels and victories among the Jews—I won't be bound by my own nature."

Mild and flawless Mary smiled and with her small white hand stroked Jesus' brow in a gesture of permission. So Jesus left the company of the Virgin and her angels and abandoned his divine form. His Mother gave him a pair of soft gray leathery wings, and a compact furry body with strong haunches and gloved forepaws like a raccoon's. In the form of a ciclogriff, with his divine eyes gazing from above the severe beak of an eagle, Jesus flew down to earth.

He flew down through the cool aethereal stars of heaven and past the fiery material stars of creation, and down through the clouds of a night sky over the North Sea. The black ocean churned and tilted under him. Swells of wind caught his wings and sent him careening through the night. Jesus felt the cold air split over his clenched beak, riffling through his fur, and the joyful pulse of risk and adventure was restored in him. With unfaltering wing strokes he brought himself down to the tower over the surf where Isolt stood at the railing wrapped in her cloak, looking out over the waves.

At first Isolt thought that the creature flapping down to her side was a seabird blown from its perch, or a bat from its cave in the cliffs that rose beachless from the waves. The ciclogriff shuddered water from its outspread wings and folded them around its body. Then like a tame rabbit it hopped quietly to Isolt's side. When the creature laid its beak against her knee and stretched its neck to look up into her face, Isolt petted it. She let her hand rest on the ciclogriff's round furry head, and with a finger traced the cool surface of his beak, while she looked out at the water where Tristram had sailed.

•   •   •

In many of the oldest illustrations of the story of Tristram and Isolt, the ciclogriff can be seen in this pose, his head resting against the side of Isolt's leg. In some representations, he stares back at the viewer with bold intelligence. In some he is portrayed, inaccurately, with birdlike webbed feet or claws rather than furry paws. Because of the batlike wings visible in all versions, and the handlike forepaws, some scholars have taken the figure of the ciclogriff to signify the spirits of Hell to which the lovers are doomed, or a mystic familiar, a symbol of the magical powers Isolt inherited from her mother.

That the little creature was in fact a latter incarnation of our Saviour Jesus Christ was not revealed even to Isolt herself, although the ciclogriff did often speak to her, during their many long nights together, of his days among the Jews in the time of Jesus. In Cornwall and in Wales and even as a child in Ireland, she had seen Jewish peddlers and scribes. Jewish settlements were common in the south and west of Britain, dark warrens of huts and workshops where the Jews sold trinkets and precious gems, rare manuscripts and absurd ballads. For Isolt, the Jews were exotic creatures like Gypsies, and in childhood lore the descendants of the betrayers of Jesus.

The ciclogriff spoke to Isolt of political and religious factions in the dynasties of the Herods and the Maccabees, of the struggles between the Pharisees and the Sadducees, and of King Herod Antipas's ploys to appear sufficiently Jewish in the eyes of the populace. He told her of the bottomless intrigues amongst the families of the ten wives of Herod the Great, the incests and fratricides and infanticides and parricides in the great ruling houses, Jewish and part Jewish and Pagan. By the fire at night, or through the long afternoons in the palace of King Mark, always within earshot of the thundering and sighing waves, Isolt thinking constantly of Tristram distracted herself with the strange stories of the ciclogriff.

In turn, Jesus asked Isolt about the movements and sensations of romantic love. First, shy even in the presence of the little beaked creature, she told him about the intertwining of love and wounds. She recounted the story of how Tristram arrived in Ireland by ship, with his harp and his wound, and how Isolt's mother the sorceress nursed him to health, only to find the chipped place in Tristram's sword that matched the fragment that was embedded in the brainpan of Sir Marhaus the brother of Isolt's mother and the champion of Ireland.

The ciclogriff looked up at Isolt with his grave intelligent eyes, and she told him about Tristram's harp and his voice. She told him about Tristram's reckless courage in battle, the terrible gashes and punctures he had sustained by sword and by lance, his deep honor and his disdain for public glory. She told the story of the Irish dragon that terrified her home country and that nearly killed Tristram, who finally cut off the monster's head and left it smoking on the ground, taking with him only the dragon's black tongue that he cut off as a trophy. The Seneschal found the dragon's head and carried it into court claiming that he had severed it in battle. The Seneschal was exposed and shamed when the missing tongue was found hanging by a silver chain from Tristram's armor, along with a bit of blue ribbon from Isolt's gown.

For nearly a year the ciclogriff remained in Cornwall attending Isolt, walking the ramparts with her or talking in her chamber, where she kept herself apart from King Mark. Because God the Father had made Jesus love all humankind with a boundless and impartial mercy, the ciclogriff could not fall in love with the fair Isolt, but he was moved by the passionate and confused course of her life, by her beauty, and by the artless, obsessive way she told her story. He amused her and shocked her with his stories of the cunning and ambitious generals and whores and priests of Judaea. Once, Isolt thought to ask him if he had seen our Lord and Saviour Jesus Christ.

"I was there," said the ciclogriff, "at His trial and at his Mortification. I was there when they crucified Him."

As always, it was impossible to tell from Isolt's face and voice if she believed what the ciclogriff said. "When they put the crown of thorns on His head," she asked, "and when they mocked Him and scourged Him?"

"Yes."

"And what was the bearing of Our Lord, what did you read in His face?"

"He knew them. He knew them through and through, Jew, Roman and Greek. Jesus was like someone who has already won the contest or stored up his profit. He was the Victor, and as the Victor He pitied them."

As Isolt grew less shy, she told the ciclogriff in detail about the pleasures and hurts of love between a man and a woman. She described how two people become as one, without shame or concealment. Over the months she recounted the trysts and separations, the vows and losses, of her life with Tristram. For all this Jesus felt pity, but also a gratifying sense of reliving his own drama, the struggle for which he had come. In Isolt's almost childish accounts of the effects upon her of the love potion she had swallowed, in the heedless contradictions and paradoxes of the behavior of the two lovers in Isolt's own account, the Son of Man felt something that eased the restlessness of his own double nature. At times, it was as if he walked the streets of Jerusalem again, defying the Sanhedrin by curing the blind on the Sabbath.

•   •   •

Then one day Tristram appeared, and carried Isolt away. Like a storm from the sea he sailed up one morning and broke through the castle's defenses, and leaving a trail of blood he carried her away as he had before. The ciclogriff awoke to the cries of the wounded and the agitated sounds of the castle resounding to King Mark's helpless rage. Jesus took wing immediately. From the bright, icy height of a cloudless sky he spotted the sails of Tristram's ship. Within minutes he was on board, and in the cabin of the lovers.

When Jesus Christ, in the shape of the ciclogriff, first looked on Tristram of Lyonesse, Tristram was thirty-eight years of age, a tall, bull-necked and scar-covered killer and harper. Tristram was wearing a sleeveless linen sleeping gown cut off at his battlemarked thighs, which resembled the twisted and mutilated boles of a double oak. Tristram's yellow hair, streaked with gray, fell to his shoulders. One scar crossed his boyish face from his left temple to the corner of his mouth, and his body was a maze of puckered lines and pale indentations. In his arms was a blue harp.

Tristram had been playing and singing to Isolt when the sailors brought Jesus to his cabin, and he resumed singing almost immediately. In a sweet high tenor, almost a counter tenor, Tristram sang the improbable and violent stories of chivalry. In the course of his first time on earth, Jesus had known many soldiers and violent men: professional killers, practical thieves, uncontrolled brutes. But nothing in that adult, Romanized world prepared him for the solemnly choreographed, pedantically structured brutality of chivalric combat. The boyish code of knighthood fascinated the Saviour, with its heroes who hacked at one another all afternoon, according to rules immutable as the musical scales, making the ground slippery with blood, and then kissed and swore promises and escorted one another to chapels to be confessed by suffragans.

Isolt listened calmly, her head resting on Tristram's chest and one hand toying with the long fur at the ciclogriff's nape, her matchless face full of contentment, while the knight sang in his high voice of his bloody battles with Sir Palamides, the sad strokes they each received, the blows that brought them bleeding to one knee or groveling to the earth, the challenges and maimings and courtesies. The ciclogriff, with his experience of triumph in the receiving of blows, listened with strange compassion to the grave, sweet self-celebrations of Tristram, doomed to defeat and loss in his skill at the giving of blows.

Conversely, all that the ciclogriff told of the intrigues and abominations of Judaea Tristram converted into poems of lofty and stylized combat. The intricate, subtle treachery of Herod Antipas, the hypocrisies bequeathed by Marc Antony to corrupt governors and wheedling catamites, perfected by rulers who as a matter of policy assassinated their sons and wives and mothers and grandmothers, Tristram took from the hooked beak of the ciclogriff and returned as highminded, repetitious lays and poems of preposterous beauty. Sir Antipas and Lady Herodias and Sir Pontius Pilate himself were led by the harp of Tristram through the naïve, murderous dance of loyalty and honor. Tristram thanked the ciclogriff for bringing him new material for his poetry.

The Jewish soul of Jesus, pragmatic, ethical, logical, found in the passionate and self-defeating codes of romantic love and knightly combat some of what he lacked in the jeweled pavilions of Heaven. He sailed with Tristram and Isolt to the far coast of Ireland and the Gard Obscure. Tristram trained the ciclogriff to skip and dart over the mighty two-edged sword as Tristram whirled and flashed it through the air. Two or three times, at jousts and tournaments, Jesus rode in a velvet pouch slung from Isolt's sidesaddle, and watched Tristram put aside the blue harp in order to maim and butcher the flower of Irish youth—from horseback with his lance, or on foot with sword and mace.

Once, Tristram returned from an expedition, half raid and half courtly gesture, to a neighboring fiefdom. The knight was exhilarated and wounded, blood pumping through his chainmail from a deep gash in his side. Isolt bathed the wound in barkwater and dressed it with herbs and linen. The next day the hero, still a little feverish and overexcited, came limping into Isolt's chamber, harp in hand, and found the ciclogriff on her lap. Playfully, Tristram cuffed at the little creature with his free hand. The ciclogriff raised its dainty paw and caught Tristram's wrist, arresting the blow with the strength of an iron bar. Tristram looked thoughtfully into the calm, intelligent gaze of Jesus for a moment. Then he shrugged, like a man who has stepped on his dog's tail, causing it to growl.

That day, Tristram sang his poem of the brothers Sir Helios and Sir Helakos, who fell upon Sir Palamides, cursing him as a Saracen and the two attacking him both at once. And Sir Palamides said that he trusted to die as good a Christian man as either brother, and that either they or he should be left dead in that place. And they rode over him, and lashed him many sad blows back and forth, until desperately he struck Sir Helakos dead through his shield. And then Sir Helios waxed strong, and doubled his strokes, and drove Sir Palamides endlong down the field and onto one knee, before the people of the city, who marveled that after so many wounds Sir Palamides could stand even on his knee. And hearing the people of the city, Sir Palamides spoke shame to himself, and lunged up and struck Sir Helios in the grated visage of his armor so that he fell to the ground groveling, whereat Sir Palamides darted up to him lightly and lashed off his helmet and smote him a blow that parted his head from his body.

·　　·　　·

A few weeks after Tristram sang this poem in praise of his old enemy Palamides, before the fair Isolt and Our Lord Jesus Christ in the shape of a ciclogriff, Tristram and Isolt were parted for the last time in life. Tristram left the Gard Obscure at the request of Arthur, and King Mark came and took what was his. The ciclogriff sailed with Isolt back to Tintagil, where he had first found her, and he would have liked to have talked as in the old days. But though she was affectionate, and kept the creature near her, Isolt took on a new custom of prolonged silences. In silence, while she stood at the rail or sat by the fire apart from the King, the ciclogriff held his beak at her knee in the old way.

Then one day word came that Sir Tristram was sick, and Isolt with a grant from Arthur that King Mark dare not deny sailed with her poultices and herbs to try to heal him as he had been healed by the arts of her mother years before. When she came into the room where Tristram lay dead by spite and trickery, the ciclogriff padded briskly at Isolt's heels. He remained at her side as she pressed a last kiss on the scar that crossed Tristram's face, and fell dead herself.

When Tristram and Isolt came together to the Gates of Hell, the ciclogriff was trotting at her side. He looked up at the towering ebony gates, the carved posts wider than five men could span, the black doors like tall cliffs, carved all over with obscenities and tortures, putti brutalized by centaurs, aged rabbis forced by centurions to defile the Torah, the mass boilings and incinerations of the damned, packed writhing into kettles and ovens. Jesus could see the seams and mends in the doors where he had burst the gates apart when he went down into the depths and harrowed the infernal spirits. He smiled to see that Satan had improvised ornamental buttresses and scenes of atrocity to cover the cracks where the gateposts of Hell had burst under the Saviour's blows.

Then Jesus turned to Isolt where she and Tristram stood before the gates and shed his form of a ciclogriff and revealed himself to her as he was in the garden of Gethsemane. With his human hand he stayed her and he told Tristram and Isolt that he was their Lord and Saviour Jesus Christ, who had been with them in the false shape of the ciclogriff. Urgently he called them to renounce their false attachments and their sins, and to follow him into the Kingdom of Heaven. In his clipped, all but cryptic manner of old, the Son of Man spoke hurriedly of the confusions and half-truths of their lives. Shedding tears of compassion, he lifted his hand to heal their blindness, and the hand glowed as if on fire, and his tears glowed, throwing the mysterious light of his truth over the Gates of Hell.

Isolt showed no surprise when the ciclogriff revealed himself as the Lord Jesus, though he felt that she listened intently to his words. Her beauty appeared more profound in the light of his raised hand and his tears. She seemed about to respond to Jesus, but the gates opened and Tristram deep in the habit of his old ways had already turned impatiently to descend into the fiery pit, with his foolish harp in his hand and his immense, futile sword hanging at his side. Instantly Isolt took his hand and they went down together into the pit.

•　　　•　　　•

The Gates of Hell banged shut and Jesus with nothing else to do turned his back on them. He climbed up through the deep caves of the earth and through the burning planets and stars of the material world. He looked down as he passed over Tintagil in Cornwall and the Gard Obscure in the West of

Ireland, and in the Holy Land over Nazareth and Galilee, and over Golgotha, the Place of Skulls. He flew on, up through the cool eternal stars of Heaven, until he reached the throne of his Mother, the Holy Virgin. There he looked into the mild eyes of Mary, who looked back with heavenly pity at the Son of Man, the most unfortunate of all his Father's creatures.

IMMORTAL LONGINGS

Inside the silver body
Slowing as it banks through veils of cloud
We float separately in our seats

Like the cells or atoms of one
Creature, needs
And states of a shuddering god.

Under him, a thirsty brilliance.
Pulsing or steady,
The fixed lights of the city

And the flood of carlights coursing
Through the grid: Delivery,
Arrival, Departure. Whim. Entering

And entered. Touching
And touched: down
The lit boulevards, over the bridges

And the river like an arm of night.
Book, cigarette. Bathroom.
Thirst. Some of us are asleep.

We tilt roaring
Over the glittering
Zodiac of intentions.

EXILE

Every few years you move
From one city to another
As if to perform this ritual.
Pictures to arrange, and furniture,

Cartons of books to shelve—
And here, bundled in newspaper,
Memory's mortal tokens, treasure
Of a life unearthed:

Clouded honey, seizures
Of hopelessness and passion,
Good nights or bad ones,
Days of minor victories and scars

Tasting of silver or iron.
Touch, loss, shouts, arts,
Gestures, whispers,
Helpless violence of sensation

Like rain flailing a window—
Then a clap of light, the body blinded
You could not say whether by
Restitution or disaster,

Clarified by tears and thunder.
Now you begin. For an instant
Everything reassures you
The long exile is over.

AN OLD MAN

AFTER CAVAFY

Back in a corner, alone in the clatter and babble
An old man sits with his head bent over a table
And his newspaper in front of him, in the café.

Sour with old age, he ponders a dreary truth—
How little he enjoyed the years when he had youth,
Good looks and strength and clever things to say.

He knows he's quite old now: he feels it, he sees it,
And yet the time when he was young seems—was it?
Yesterday. How quickly, how quickly it slipped away.

Now he sees how Discretion has betrayed him,
And how stupidly he let the liar persuade him
With phrases: *Tomorrow. There's plenty of time. Some day.*

He recalls the pull of impulses he suppressed,
The joy he sacrificed. Every chance he lost
Ridicules his brainless prudence a different way.

But all these thoughts and memories have made
The old man dizzy. He falls asleep, his head
Resting on the table in the noisy café.

WHAT WHY WHEN HOW WHO

The lovers love the boardwalk, the games of chance
And the cheap bright treats, booths and indifferent surf,
The old conspiracy of gain and pleasure

Flowering in the mind greedily to build the world
And break it. In the city, steel cords twitch a girder
Onto its fittings as the tower grows

Amid a pool of dwellings made from its litter—
Crate or abandoned dumpster, some built with reckless
Improvisation framelessly from tires,

Scrapwood and hammered cans. One room or dormer
Is a gutted TV set: a hollowed console
Large enough for a body, with a curtain

Hung neatly in the screen. Somewhere but where
Inside this body, infinitesimal keys
Brush over their tumblers in the oily dark

To stir the mysteries, Love and Work, we have made
And that make us willing to die for them—
That make us bleed, embodied maybe in codes,

Spurts of pressure and crucial variations
In the current of the soul, that lives by changing.
He liked her knees, her taste and smell. She thought

About the night they walked home over the snow,
The sound of presence itself crunching and squeaking
Under their boots in the abandoned streets,

Their bodies under their coats when they stopped to hug.
What do the lovers want? And we, do we prefer
The ocean or the snow? Or page sixteen

Of *Naughty Nurses?* What is it we need to feel
The other feels, to fill our wants? One man
Wanted to have a woman while she was drowning,

To have her feel him inside her when she drowned,
So when his family were away, he killed
A woman he paid, bound helpless in the tub.

We can enrich the scene around the crane
By imagining a lunchtime song and dance:
A gang of children from the shanties perform

To a tape machine, dancing and chanting along
An octave higher to supplement the machine's
Overworked speaker. Its regular distortion

Pulses like drumbrushes as they shuffle and skip,
Swinging their hips and clapping. A key keeps turning,
The tumblers falling to their inertial state:

Heavy equipment will clear away the warrens
That stream around the Cyclone fence, to grow
Again like weeds; though for now the builders applaud

And pass a few dollars through the silver fence
From where they eat their sandwiches in the shade
While the children caper. Or say the lovers smile

And give them money too, because it charms them
Or pleases us. The poor whore only wanted
The money, she was young, she meant to live.

But now a camera charms us, it has caught
Ballplayers miming instruments in the dugout:
One tootling a bat held out like a clarinet,

One strumming, another puffing a bat-bassoon,
The uniformed players playing, as in a Bacchic
Procession. When we buried the old man,

To do it right we had to stop seven times
As we walked toward the grave, to lower the body
Inside its box down to rest on the earth

And pray and lift it up again, each prayer
Functioning as a pause by which to show
Our sevenfold resistance, refusing haste.

And when we mourners do the actual work
Of shoveling the earth in, each taking a turn
With the one shovel, we must not pass the shovel

From hand to hand, but take it standing from earth
And shovel, then stab it back to where it stood.
The lovers live by the exacting rules

And discipline of their folly, they are without
Earnestness or hypocrisy, they are useless.
They don't say anything about the poor,

Or exchange scorn for the President, they are like
The dying poet who could not fix his attention
On approaching World War II, because he felt

Distracted by a girl. They cannot pay attention
To their food, whole centuries of suffering children
Are as nothing to them, and even while they speak

They barely listen, but trembling scribble an image
Of one another inside, stanzas or cartoons.
Even at the end of the world each lover searches

The eyes in the mirror of eyes to find an object
That is still snagged far down among the dark
Roots that grow tangled in the bottomless wells

Of our invention, the waters that pull downward
And drink up every motion of mind and body,
Agonized hunger for What Why When How Who—

More images, as when desiring we desire
Fresh musics of desire, at concentric removes.
Doing a brake job, he sings into the wheel

Somewhere alone she knows a boy is waiting
Ta da ta da ta da, So she drives on through
The night anticipating, because he makes

Her feel the way she used to feel, and so
While he rebuilds the calipers he makes
Me feel the music of her heart as she

Drives toward the boy whose waiting she imagines
Restoring her lost desire, concentric rings
Each seeing more than the one that it encloses

Yet somehow larger than what we make around it,
With even the death camps radiating their jargon
And nicknames, surrounded by their lore and studies

As the tumblers fall. The current swells and shifts,
It lives by changing—Andreas Capellanus
Eight hundred years ago, *The Art of Love:*

Rule IV: *It is well known that love is always
Increasing or decreasing.* The country changes
Outside of town, and the little town itself

Is so demolished it seems that all along
It was a tissue of changes, though the boardwalk
Still with its giddy herringbone ribbon marks

Our element at its border with a greater one,
That in its darkness regularly roars
And falls and rises: as if we made a rocket

Molded in the image of a human body
Hugging its shoulders, head at the streaming prow
With eyes held shut, and launched it at the sun.

VOYAGE TO THE MOON

"Aggression: the strife of desire; the monstrous overbuilding of the imagination; all the maze of displacement and sublimation—if the soul in its fatigue should conceive some arcadia devoid of all this fevered construction, then our first footstep there would infect and repopulate that lunar terrain."

Raquel the Queen of Diamonds and La Hire
The One-Eyed Jack of Hearts have crossed a bridge
Of weathered stone, from the Old Town to the New,

Which is itself so old the houses lean
Drowsily under their crowns of thatch. They have
Coffee on the terrace of an inn that looks

Out over the canal: lawn, ducks, the towpath,
And in the distance beyond the hilly streets,
Turrets and pennants, and puffs of cloud. The pack

Of cards in their expectant, somewhat embarrassed
Silence are waiting for what will happen next,
Or for the story to go deeper in—

La Hire with his painted hatchet and leaf, Raquel
With her bouquet of poppies. There was a woman
Who worked in sweatshops or sewing piecework at home

To support her daughter and herself. The child
Spent hours alone inventing games of cards
Based on Casino and the Death of Arthur,

Or on Disney, the brothers Grimm and the game of War.
She gave them voices, and played against herself.
And later when she grew up and was a sculptor

She made a series of works with heavy limbs
Of smooth black metal, muscled and stenciled gold
With leaves and filigrees like the stiff black arm

Of her mother's old-fashioned sewing machine.
And one work in particular was titled
La Blaine du Var, after her favorite card,

A little dog portrayed by the Three of Spades
And named in the private French the child invented.
Raquel and her friend Argine the Queen of Clubs

Had won the dog in a struggle with Oscarre,
The Suicide King who holds his sword at his head:
She gave his name to an eight-foot work with chrome

Sinews and targets welded among the tangle
Of gilded black. Meanwhile the pair of court cards
Have clambered into the wicker gondola,

Already they are lifted above the earth
By the silken gaudy bulb of a balloon
Painted in the yellow and red of their brocades

With arcs of scallops, and lozenges of blue.
They steer it with a treadle and a fan.
But the cards were flat, their passion to be lifted

Became too light for her, she wanted the earth
Made sweeter by the feel of the weight that presses
Against it when it comes back down, she studied

The languorous gestures of the dying deposed
Dictator in his American hospital bed,
Smiling at the camera the way that Mordred smiled

Impaled on his father Arthur's spear, the Knights
All fallen, all ruin. And Mordred lifting his sword
Ran the spear's length that pierced him, and dying gave Arthur

The Dolorous Wound. The four Queens on the barge,
Argine and Palas, Morgana and Raquel,
Took Arthur aboard and away in the windy dusk.

The Queens were afraid his wound had grown too cold.
Then robbers and pillers came into the field
To take the rings and brooches and lady's favors

From off the bodies of the noble knights.
"And who were not dead all out, there they slew
To get their harness and their riches." She got

The words by heart, the noble story daring
To pillage its corpses from outside itself:
Because it could, because the loss was richer

If the world could go on ending endlessly—
Who are these pillagers, neither knight nor squire,
Like readers who enter the story at the end

Only to be read in turn, as dynasties fall
With new inheritors to loot the shell
Of each catastrophe?—the heavy balloon

Of passion escaping from the earth, but thudding
Back to transform it, like the philosopher
Who said that he could move the world itself

If he had somewhere he could stand outside it.
World without end: fifty-two weeks or cards,
But always waiting outside the deck or the year

Pillagers and witnesses, a perpetual fall:
The black captain strangles his wife, and we
In the pack applaud and applaud, the sound of our hands

In a fluttering mass around that heavy act
As in Isaiah, when after the promised End
The blessed go forth to look upon the corpses

Of the transgressors, and "their worm shall not die
Nor their fire be quenched, they shall be an abhorring
Unto flesh forever." She made it a work

Of metal nets and pouches, a spider presence.
But in her heart she felt the foretold end
Might come more lightly, even through some absurd

Miscalculation: the feeding of penicillin
Too much to pigs, so inside those heavy bodies
Unheard-of microbes would breed and multiply

To engulf the world in plague—some giddy fate
Unlikely as a perfect hand: some trick
Of Arniboule the King of Spades, the mighty

Maker and Breaker with his crown of glass
In spikes like icicles, his violent paws
Of metal, his many arms, his orbs and swords

Doubled like his reflection in the moat
Around the palace of the Moon—where now
The pair have landed with their little dog.

SHIRT

The back, the yoke, the yardage. Lapped seams,
The nearly invisible stitches along the collar
Turned in a sweatshop by Koreans or Malaysians

Gossiping over tea and noodles on their break
Or talking money or politics while one fitted
This armpiece with its overseam to the band

Of cuff I button at my wrist. The presser, the cutter,
The wringer, the mangle. The needle, the union,
The treadle, the bobbin. The code. The infamous blaze

At the Triangle Factory in nineteen-eleven.
One hundred and forty-six died in the flames
On the ninth floor, no hydrants, no fire escapes—

The witness in a building across the street
Who watched how a young man helped a girl to step
Up to the windowsill, then held her out

Away from the masonry wall and let her drop.
And then another. As if he were helping them up
To enter a streetcar, and not eternity.

A third before he dropped her put her arms
Around his neck and kissed him. Then he held
Her into space, and dropped her. Almost at once

He stepped to the sill himself, his jacket flared
And fluttered up from his shirt as he came down,
Air filling up the legs of his gray trousers—

Like Hart Crane's Bedlamite, "shrill shirt ballooning."
Wonderful how the pattern matches perfectly
Across the placket and over the twin bar-tacked

Corners of both pockets, like a strict rhyme
Or a major chord. Prints, plaids, checks,
Houndstooth, Tattersall, Madras. The clan tartans

Invented by mill-owners inspired by the hoax of Ossian,
To control their savage Scottish workers, tamed
By a fabricated heraldry: MacGregor,

Bailey, MacMartin. The kilt, devised for workers
To wear among the dusty clattering looms.
Weavers, carders, spinners. The loader,

The docker, the navvy. The planter, the picker, the sorter
Sweating at her machine in a litter of cotton
As slaves in calico headrags sweated in fields:

George Herbert, your descendant is a Black
Lady in South Carolina, her name is Irma
And she inspected my shirt. Its color and fit

And feel and its clean smell have satisfied
Both her and me. We have culled its cost and quality
Down to the buttons of simulated bone,

The buttonholes, the sizing, the facing, the characters
Printed in black on neckband and tail. The shape,
The label, the labor, the color, the shade. The shirt.

THE NIGHT GAME

Some of us believe
We would have conceived romantic
Love out of our own passions
With no precedents,
Without songs and poetry—
Or have invented poetry and music
As a comb of cells for the honey.

Shaped by ignorance,
A succession of new worlds,
Congruities improvised by
Immigrants or children.

I once thought most people were Italian,
Jewish or Colored.
To be white and called
Something like *Ed Ford*
Seemed aristocratic,
A rare distinction.

Possibly I believed only gentiles
And blonds could be left-handed.

Already famous
After one year in the majors,
Whitey Ford was drafted by the Army
To play ball in the flannels
Of the Signal Corps, stationed
In Long Branch, New Jersey.

A night game, the silver potion
Of the lights, his pink skin
Shining like a burn.

Never a player
I liked or hated: a Yankee,
A mere success.

But white the chalked-off lines
In the grass, white and green
The immaculate uniform,
And white the unpigmented
Halo of his hair
When he shifted his cap:

So ordinary and distinct,
So close up, that I felt
As if I could have made him up,
Imagined him as I imagined

The ball, a scintilla
High in the black backdrop
Of the sky. Tight red stitches.
Rawlings. The bleached

Horsehide white: the color
Of nothing. Color of the past
And of the future, of the movie screen
At rest and of blank paper.

"*I could have.*" The mind. The black
Backdrop, the white
Fly picked out by the towering
Lights. A few years later

On a blanket in the grass
By the same river
A girl and I came into
Being together
To the faint muttering
Of unthinkable
Troubadours and radios.

The emerald
Theater, the night.
Another time,
I devised a left-hander

Even more gifted
Than Whitey Ford: a Dodger.
People were amazed by him.
Once, when he was young,
He refused to pitch on Yom Kippur.

SONNET

Afternoon sun on her back,
calm irregular slap
of water against a dock.

Thin pines clamber
over the hill's top—
nothing to remember,

only the same lake
that keeps making the same
sounds under her cheek

and flashing the same color.
No one to say her name,
no need, no one to praise her,

only the lake's voice—over
and over, to keep it before her.

DREAMER

While I lay sleeping my heart awoke.
I heard and saw but I couldn't stir.
He walked out like a man and spoke.
Though it was late
A crowd of people were awake
Strolling and talking in the street.
They greeted him and called him Coeur.
Then he was driving in a car.

He started down familiar roads.
I know the city, he was there,
But Coeur found hidden neighborhoods.
At an iron gate
That led to steps between façades
I watched him park and climb on foot
The passage to an open square
With shuttered houses and a bar,

A bright café where I could see
Coeur chatting with the local crowd—
Voluble heart, attentive, free,
At home, at night.
Once I think he looked back at me
And for a moment saw me wait
(I saw his face, he looked afraid)
Dreaming him from the dark outside.

THE REFINERY

". . . our language, forged in the dark by centuries of violent pressure, underground, out of the stuff of dead life."

Thirsty and languorous after their long black sleep
The old gods crooned and shuffled and shook their heads.
Dry, dry. By railroad they set out
Across the desert of stars to drink the world
Our mouths had soaked
In the strange sentences we made
While they were asleep: a pollen-tinted
Slurry of passion and lapsed
Intention, whose imagined
Taste made the savage deities hiss and snort.

In the lightless carriages, a smell of snake
And coarse fur, glands of lymphless breath
And ichor, the avid stenches of
Immortal bodies.

Their long train clicked and sighed
Through the gulfs of night between the planets
And came down through the evening fog
Of redwood canyons. From the train
At sunset, fiery warehouse windows
Along a wharf. Then dusk, a gash of neon:
Bar. Black pinewoods, a junction crossing, glimpses
Of sluggish surf among the rocks, a moan
Of dreamy forgotten divinity calling and fading
Against the windows of a town. Inside
The train, a flash
Of dragonfly wings, an antlered brow.

Black night again, and then
After the bridge, a palace on the water:

The great Refinery—impossible city of lights,
A million bulbs tracing its turreted
Boulevards and mazes. The castle of a person

Pronounced alive, the Corporation: a fictional
Lord real in law.

Barbicans and torches
Along the siding where the engine slows
At the central tanks, a ward
Of steel palisades, valved and chandeliered.

The muttering gods
Greedily penetrate those bright pavilions—
Libation of Benzene, Naphthalene, Asphalt,
Gasoline, Tar: syllables
Fractioned and cracked from unarticulated

Crude, the smeared keep of life that fed
On itself in pitchy darkness when the gods
Were new—inedible, volatile
And sublimated afresh to sting
Our tongues who use it, refined from oil of stone.

The gods batten on the vats, and drink up
Lovecries and memorized Chaucer, lines from movies
And songs hoarded in mortmain: exiles' charms,
The basal or desperate distillates of breath
Steeped, brewed and spent
As though we were their aphids, or their bees,
That monstered up sweetness for them while they dozed.

HUT

Nothing only
what it was—

Slates, burls, rims:

Their names like the circus
Lettering on a van: *Bros.* and *Movers*,
Symmetrical buds of
Meaning in the spurs and serifs
Of scarlet with gold outlines.

Transport and Salvage,
Moving and Storage.

The house by the truck yard:
Flag walk. Shake siding. The frontyard spruce
A hilt of shadows.

And out back in the wooded lot,
The hut of scrapwood and bedframes
Lashed with housewire by children,
Hitchknots of the plainsman
Or the plasterer shoring a ladder.

Cache of cigarettes, tongue
And groove, magazines,
Chocolate, books: *Moaning she guided*
His throbbing manhood and *Southwark Bridge*
Which is of iron
And London Bridge which is of stone.

Hobo cookery in tin cans.
Muffled coherence like dreams.

Printslugs,
Glass insulators, "Enemy Zeros."
Maimed mouth-harp and sashweight.
Trojans and Sheiks,

Esquire,
Beaverboard, Romex.
Each thing or name a river
With a silty bottom.
The source hidden, the mouth
Emptying in the ocean.

Hut as of driftwood,
Scavengers and Haulers,
Household and Commercial Removals.
Westphal's Auxiliator, *quim, poorhouse,*
Homasote,

The mighty forest of significance—
Possibly dreamed
By a man in Headlight overalls,
Even by the one we found
Sleeping there once
With his empty of Seven
Crown, not necessarily
By a god or goddess—
The embroidered letters
HEAD tapering each smaller and LIGHT
Each larger, like beams thrown
From the center—that snoring,
Historical heart.

THE GHOST HAMMER

Foundry of the dead, the dead invisible hammer
Forgotten that dropped to forge
The ring behind the doorknob: brass roses
The trade tongue calls them, and forges the words—
Tongue, strike-plate, shaft, escutcheon, exhaling tarnish
Onto your hand that reaches unknowing toward them
Over and over in doorways and all but touches.

Shaft and claw, clangor and fission:
The brazen tongue of Babylon.

The faint implacable hammer behind the hammer
Homing the die and bevel and framing the house.

Hammerdust air, a contagious powder of blows.

Mattock that breaks the earth.
Sacrifice, felling the housel.

At the window
Where children are walking home from school it showers
Around their heads: the burst of particles that spray
Up from the anvil unnoticed over the children
And onto the window—sash, lights, mullion and sill,
Molecules that gild the panes and film the moist
Pupil of the eye with ashy silver.

Airhammer in the street
Tireless and violent in a fissure
Of pavement. Warhammer of Tristram or Shiva.

Old hammer of mortal perfection, idolatrous hammer
Of golden calves and birds, the shingle maker
Wielding his maul and froe, dead jeweler's hammer
Forcing a braid of silver into the vessels

Of living bodies, heartworm
Tendrils and cilia. Shapes taken out of nature
In wires of laurel or olive. Roses.

Pounding: the bell-shaped strokes.

Oh heavy swollen pump, the urgent pressure
Lifted in desire.

Hammer of love hammered by the hammer of words.

Futile the prophet Ezekiel's curse on the sledge
Hefted by the weary idol-smith who works
Hypnotized faint with hunger beyond his supper
By lamplight, thirsty, and beyond his death
Lifting the ponderous shaper.

In his anger
Ezekiel said to smear the bread in the ovens
With Babylonian shit, as a mouth penance
For graving images, but the very baker
Pounded and pounded the dough and twisted the
Ropes of the bread of affliction
Into crown-shaped loaves.

Braids, images.

Blind tool of perfection, bludgeon
Handed from the dead who drive you
Hand on the doorknob between Sheol and Creation,
Stalled on the threshold, unable to cross.

Pounding of the heart,
Inherited drum of the doorway.

Mattock of want, sickle of Kali, bare hand
Of hunger—you too have lifted it and let it fall,
You have committed images, the tool
Is warm from your hand.

AT PLEASURE BAY

In the willows along the river at Pleasure Bay
A catbird singing, never the same phrase twice.
Here under the pines a little off the road
In 1927 the Chief of Police
And Mrs. W. killed themselves together,
Sitting in a roadster. Ancient unshaken pilings
And underwater chunks of still-mortared brick
In shapes like bits of puzzle strew the bottom
Where the landing was for Price's Hotel and Theater.
And here's where boats blew two blasts for the keeper
To shunt the iron swing-bridge. He leaned on the gears
Like a skipper in the hut that housed the works
And the bridge moaned and turned on its middle pier
To let them through. In the middle of the summer
Two or three cars might wait for the iron trusswork
Winching aside, with maybe a child to notice
A name on the stern in black-and-gold on white,
Sandpiper, Patsy Ann, Do Not Disturb,
The Idler. If a boat was running whiskey,
The bridge clanged shut behind it as it passed
And opened up again for the Coast Guard cutter
Slowly as a sundial, and always jammed halfway.
The roadbed whole, but opened like a switch,
The river pulling and coursing between the piers.
Never the same phrase twice, the catbird filling
The humid August evening near the inlet
With borrowed music that he melds and changes.
Dragonflies and sandflies, frogs in the rushes, two bodies
Not moving in the open car among the pines,
A sliver of story. The tenor at Price's Hotel,
In clown costume, unfurls the sorrow gathered
In ruffles at his throat and cuffs, high quavers
That hold like splashes of light on the dark water,
The aria's closing phrases, changed and fading.
And after a gap of quiet, cheers and applause

Audible in the houses across the river,
Some in the audience weeping as if they had melted
Inside the music. Never the same. In Berlin
The daughter of an English lord, in love
With Adolf Hitler, whom she has met. She is taking
Possession of the apartment of a couple,
Elderly well-off Jews. They survive the war
To settle here in the Bay, the old lady
Teaches piano, but the whole world swivels
And gapes at their feet as the girl and a high-up Nazi
Examine the furniture, the glass, the pictures,
The elegant story that was theirs and now
Is a part of hers. A few months later the English
Enter the war and she shoots herself in a park,
An addled, upper-class girl, her life that passes
Into the lives of others or into a place.
The taking of lives—the Chief and Mrs. W.
Took theirs to stay together, as local ghosts.
Last flurries of kisses, the revolver's barrel,
Shivers of a story that a child might hear
And half remember, voices in the rushes,
A singing in the willows. From across the river,
Faint quavers of music, the same phrase twice and again,
Ranging and building. Over the high new bridge
The flashing of traffic homeward from the racetrack,
With one boat chugging under the arches, outward
Unnoticed through Pleasure Bay to the open sea.
Here's where the people stood to watch the theater
Burn on the water. All that night the fireboats
Kept playing their spouts of water into the blaze.
In the morning, smoking pilasters and beams.
Black smell of char for weeks, the ruin already
Soaking back into the river. After you die
You hover near the ceiling above your body
And watch the mourners awhile. A few days more
You float above the heads of the ones you knew
And watch them through a twilight. As it grows darker
You wander off and find your way to the river
And wade across. On the other side, night air,
Willows, the smell of the river, and a mass
Of sleeping bodies all along the bank,
A kind of singing from among the rushes
Calling you further forward in the dark.

You lie down and embrace one body, the limbs
Heavy with sleep reach eagerly up around you
And you make love until your soul brims up
And burns free out of you and shifts and spills
Down over into that other body, and you
Forget the life you had and begin again
On the same crossing—maybe as a child who passes
Through the same place. But never the same way twice.
Here in the daylight, the catbird in the willows,
The new café, with a terrace and a landing,
Frogs in the cattails where the swing-bridge was—
Here's where you might have slipped across the water
When you were only a presence, at Pleasure Bay.

HISTORY OF MY HEART

(1984)

I

THE FIGURED WHEEL

The figured wheel rolls through shopping malls and prisons,
Over farms, small and immense, and the rotten little downtowns.
Covered with symbols, it mills everything alive and grinds
The remains of the dead in the cemeteries, in unmarked graves and oceans.

Sluiced by salt water and fresh, by pure and contaminated rivers,
By snow and sand, it separates and recombines all droplets and grains,
Even the infinite sub-atomic particles crushed under the illustrated,
Varying treads of its wide circumferential track.

Spraying flecks of tar and molten rock it rumbles
Through the Antarctic station of American sailors and technicians,
And shakes the floors and windows of whorehouses for diggers and smelters
From Bethany, Pennsylvania to a practically nameless, semi-penal New Town

In the mineral-rich tundra of the Soviet northernmost settlements.
Artists illuminate it with pictures and incised mottoes
Taken from the Ten Thousand Stories and the Register of True Dramas.
They hang it with colored ribbons and with bells of many pitches.

With paints and chisels and moving lights they record
On its rotating surface the elegant and terrifying doings
Of the inhabitants of the Hundred Pantheons of major Gods
Disposed in iconographic stations at hub, spoke and concentric bands,

And also the grotesque demi-Gods, Hopi gargoyles and Ibo dryads.
They cover it with wind-chimes and electronic instruments
That vibrate as it rolls to make an all-but-unthinkable music,
So that the wheel hums and rings as it turns through the births of stars

And through the dead-world of bomb, fireblast and fallout
Where only a few doomed races of insects fumble in the smoking grasses.
It is Jesus oblivious to hurt turning to give words to the unrighteous,
And is also Gogol's feeding pig that without knowing it eats a baby chick

And goes on feeding. It is the empty armor of My Cid, clattering
Into the arrows of the credulous unbelievers, a metal suit
Like the lost astronaut revolving with his useless umbilicus
Through the cold streams, neither energy nor matter, that agitate

The cold, cyclical dark, turning and returning.
Even in the scorched and frozen world of the dead after the holocaust
The wheel as it turns goes on accreting ornaments.
Scientists and artists festoon it from the grave with brilliant

Toys and messages, jokes and zodiacs, tragedies conceived
From among the dreams of the unemployed and the pampered,
The listless and the tortured. It is hung with devices
By dead masters who have survived by reducing themselves magically

To tiny organisms, to wisps of matter, crumbs of soil,
Bits of dry skin, microscopic flakes, which is why they are called "great,"
In their humility that goes on celebrating the turning
Of the wheel as it rolls unrelentingly over

A cow plodding through car-traffic on a street in Iasi,
And over the haunts of Robert Pinsky's mother and father
And wife and children and his sweet self
Which he hereby unwillingly and inexpertly gives up, because it is

There, figured and pre-figured in the nothing-transfiguring wheel.

THE UNSEEN

In Krakow it rained, the stone arcades and cobbles
And the smoky air all soaked one penetrating color
While in an Art Nouveau café, on harp-shaped chairs,

We sat making up our minds to tour the death camp.
As we drove there the next morning past farms
And steaming wooden villages, the rain had stopped

Though the sky was still gray. A young guide explained
Everything we saw in her tender, hectoring English:
The low brick barracks; the heaped-up meticulous

Mountains of shoes, toothbrushes, hair; one cell
Where the Pope had prayed and placed flowers; logbooks,
Photographs, latrines—the whole unswallowable

Menu of immensities. It began drizzling again,
And the way we paused to open or close the umbrellas,
Hers and ours, as we went from one building to the next,

Had a formal, dwindled feeling. We felt bored
And at the same time like screaming Biblical phrases:
I am poured out like water; Thine is the day and

Thine also the night; I cannot look to see
My own right hand . . . I remembered a sleep-time game,
A willed dream I had never thought of by day before:

I am there; and granted the single power of invisibility,
Roaming the camp at will. At first I savor my mastery
Slowly by creating small phantom diversions,

Then kill kill kill kill, a detailed and strangely
Passionless inward movie: I push the man holding
The crystals down from the gas chamber roof, bludgeon

The pet collie of the Commandant's children
And in the end flush everything with a vague flood
Of fire and blood as I drift on toward sleep

In a blurred finale, like our tour's—eddying
In a downpour past the preserved gallows where
The Allies hung the Commandant, in 1947.

I don't feel changed, or even informed—in that,
It's like any other historical monument; although
It is true that I don't ever at night any more

Prowl rows of red buildings unseen, doing
Justice like an angry god to escape insomnia. And so,
O discredited Lord of Hosts, your servant gapes

Obediently to swallow various doings of us, the most
Capable of all your former creatures—we have
No shape, we are poured out like water, but still

We try to take in what won't be turned from in despair:
As if, just as we turned toward the fumbled drama
Of the religious art shop window to accuse you

Yet again, you were to slit open your red heart
To show us at last the secret of your day and also,
Because it also is yours, of your night.

THE VOLUME

Or a crippled sloop falters, about to go under
In sight of huge ritual fires along the beach
With people eating and dancing, the older children

Cantering horses parallel to the ghostlike surf.
But instead the crew nurse her home somehow,
And they make her fast and stand still shivering

In the warm circle, preserved, and they may think
Or else I have drowned, and this is the last dream.
They try never to think about the whole range and weight

Of ocean. To try to picture it is like looking down
From an immense height, the oblivious black volume.
To drown in that calamitous belly would be dying twice.

When I was small, someone might say about a delicate
Uncorroded piece of equipment, that's a sweetwater reel—
And from the sound *sweetwater*, a sense of the coarse,

Kelp-colored, chill sucking of the other,
Sour and vital: governed by the moon, or in the picture
Of the blind minotaur led by the little girl,

Walking together on the beach under the partial moon,
Past amazed fishermen furled in their hoodlike sail.
Last Easter, when the branch broke under Caroline

And the jagged stub, digging itself into her thigh as she fell,
Tore her leg open to the bone, she said she didn't want to die.
And now the scar like a streak of glare on her tan leg

Flashes when she swims. Otherwise, it might be a dream.
The sad, brutal bullhead with its milky eye tilts upward
Toward the stars painted as large as moths as the helpless

Monster strides by, his hand resting on the child's shoulder,
All only a dream, painted, like the corpse's long hair
That streams back from the dory toward the shark

Scavenging in *Brook Watson and the Shark*,
The gray-green paint mysterious as water,
The wave, the boat-hook, the white faces of the living,

The hair that shows the corpse has dreamed the picture,
It is so calm; the boat and the shark and the flowing hair
All held and preserved in the green volume of water.

THE COLD

I can't remember what I was thinking . . . the cold
Outside numbs purposes to a blur, and people
Seem to be more explicitly animal—

Stamping the snow, our visible patient breath
Around our faces. When we come inside
An air of mortal health steams up from our coats,

Blood throbbing richer in the whitest faces.
When I stop working, I feel it in a draft
Leaking in somewhere. In the hardware store—

I think because it was a time of day
When people mostly are at work—it seemed
All of the other customers were old,

A group I think of five or six . . . a vague
Memory of white hair or of elder voices,
Their heavy protective coats and gloves and boots

Holding the creature warmth around their bodies.
I think that someone talked about the weather;
It was gray, then; then brighter after noon

For an hour or two. As if half-senile already,
In a winter blank, I had the stupid thought
About old age as cozy—drugged convalescence;

A forgetful hardihood of naps and drinks;
Peaceful, without the fears, pains, operations
That make life bitterest, one hears, near the end . . .

The needle *Work* unthreaded—not misplaced.
Bitterest at its own close, the short harsh day
Does lead us to hover an extra minute or two

Inside our lighted offices and stores
With our coats buttoned, holding the keys perhaps;
Or like me, working in a room, alone,

Watching out from a window, where the wind
Lifts up the snow from loaded roofs and branches,
A cold pale smoke against the sky's darkening gray—

Watching it now, not having been out in hours,
I come up closer idly, to feel the cold,
Forgetting for a minute what I was doing.

FAERYLAND

Thin snow, and the first small pools of dusk
Start to swell from the low places of the park,

The swathe of walks, rises and plantings seeming
As it turns gray to enlarge—as if tidal,

A turbulent inlet or canal that reaches to divide
Slow dual processionals of carlights on the street,

The rare vague beacon of a bar or a store.
Shapes of brick, soiled and wet, yaw in the blur.

Elder, sullen, the small mythical folk
Gather in the scraps of dark like emigrants on a deck,

Immobile in their fur boots and absurd court finery.
They are old, old; though they stand with a straight elegance,

Their hair flutters dead-white, they have withered skin.
Between a high collar and an antic brim

The face is collapsed, or beaked like a baby bird's.
To them, our most ancient decayed hopes

Are a gross, infantile greed. The city itself,
Shoreline muffled in forgotten need and grief,

To us cold as a stone Venus in the snow, for them
Shows the ham-fisted persistence of the new-born,

Hemming them to the crossed shadows of cornice and porch,
Small darknesses of fence-weeds and streetside brush:

We make them feel mean, it has worn them out,
Watching us; they stir only randomly to mete

Some petty stroke of revenge—arbitrary, unjust,
Striking our old, ailing or oppressed

Oftener than not. An old woman in galoshes
Plods from the bus, head bent in the snow, and falls,

Bruising her hip, her bags spilled in the wet.
The Old Ones watch with small grave faces, nearly polite:

As if one of them had willed a dry sour joke, a kind of pun—
A small cruel fall, lost in a greater one.

It means nothing, no more than as if to tease her
They had soured her cow's milk, or the cat spilled a pitcher,

Costing her an hour's pleasure weeding in the heat,
Grunting among the neat furrows and mounds. Tonight,

In the cold, she moans with pursed face, stoops to the street
To collect her things. Less likely, they might

Put the fritz on the complex machines in the tower
Of offices where she works—jam an elevator

Between floors, giving stranded bosses and workers a break,
Panicking some of them, an insignificant leak

Or let in some exquisite operation bobbing
In the vast, childlike play of movement

That sends cars hissing by them in the night:
The dim city whose heedless, clouded heart

Tries them, and apes them, the filmy-looking harbor
Hard in a cold pale storm that falls all over.

THREE ON LUCK

Senior Poet

"Does anybody listen to advice?
I'll soothe myself by listening to my own:
Don't squander the success of your first book;
Now that you have a little reputation,
Be patient until you've written one as good,
Instead of rushing back to print as I did—
Too soon, with an inferior second book
That all the jackals will bite and tear to pieces.
The poet-friends I loved had better sense,
Or better luck—and harder lives, I think.
But Berryman said he wanted the good luck
To be nearly crucified. The lucky artist,
He said, gets to experience the worst—
The worst conceivable ordeal or pain
That doesn't outright kill you. Poor man, poor John.
And he didn't knock on wood. It gives me gooseflesh. . . .
One of these days, we'll have a longer visit;
I think of you and Ellen as guest-starlets,
Well-paid to cross the lobbies of life, smiling,
But never beaten up or sold or raped
Like us the real characters in the movie.
I'm sure that image would yield to something solid
Given a meal together, and time to talk."

Late Child

"I never minded having such old parents
Until now; now I'm forty, and they live
And keep on living. Seneca was right—
The greatest blessing is to be hit by lightning
Before the doctors get you. Dim, not numb,
My father has seen it all get taken away
By slow degrees—his house, then his apartment,
His furniture and gadgets and his books,

And now his wife, and everything but a room
And a half-crippled brain. If I was God,
I hope I'd have the will to use the lightning—
Instead of making extra fetuses
That keep on coming down, and live, and die.
My sisters look so old, it makes me feel
As if my own life might be over, and yet
He planted me when he was older than I am.
And when the doctor told her she was pregnant,
They celebrated; in their shoes, I wouldn't.
It wouldn't be nice to have to wield the scissors,
And say when any one life was at its peak
And ripe for striking. But if God was God,
His finger would be quicker on the trigger."

Prostate Operation

"In all those years at work I must have seen
A thousand secretaries, mostly young;
And I'm the kind of man who's popular
Around an office—though that's a different thing,
Of course, from getting them to bed. But still,
I never cheated on her: now, I can't.
I don't regret them, exactly, but I do
Find myself thinking of it as a waste.
What would I feel now, if I'd had them all?
Blaming them, maybe, for helping to wear it out?
One thing's for sure, I wouldn't still have her—
Not her. I guess I'd have to say that, no,
I don't regret them; but if we do come back,
I think I'd like to try life as a pimp
Or California lover-boy; just to see . . .
Though I suppose that if we do come back
I may have been a randy King already,
With plenty of Maids and Ladies, keeping the Queen
Quiet with extra castles, or the axe.
But that's enough of that. I'll be goddammed
If I become another impotent lecher,
One of these old boys talking and talking and talking
What he can't do—it's one life at a time."

THE NEW SADDHUS

Barefoot, in unaccustomed clouts or skirts of raw muslin,
With new tin cup, rattle or scroll held in diffident hands
Stripped of the familiar cuffs, rings, watches, the new holy-men

Avoid looking at their farewelling families, an elaborate
Feigned concentration stretched over their self-consciousness and terror,
Like small boys nervous on the first day of baseball tryouts.

Fearful exalted Coptic tradesman; Swedish trucker; Palestinian doctor;
The Irish works foreman and the Lutheran optometrist from St. Paul:
They line up smirking or scowling, feeling silly, determined,

All putting aside the finite piercing restlessness of men
Who in this world have provided for their generation: O they have
Swallowed their wives' girlhoods and their children's dentistry,

Dowries and tuitions. And grown fat with swallowing they line up
Endless as the Ganges or the piles of old newspapers at the dumps,
Which may be blankets for them now; intense and bathetic

As the founders of lodges, they will overcome fatigue, self-pity, desire,
O Lords of mystery, to stare endlessly at the sun till the last
Red retinal ghost of actual sight is burned utterly away,

And still turn eyes that see no more than the forehead can see
Daily and all day toward the first faint heat of the morning.
Ready O Lords to carry one kilo of sand more each month,

More weight and more, so the fabulous thick mortified muscles
Lurch and bulge under an impossible tonnage of stupid,
Particulate inertia, and still O Lords ready, men and not women

And not young men, but the respectable Kurd, Celt, Marxist
And Rotarian, chanting and shuffling in place a little now
Like their own pimply, reformed-addict children, as they put aside

The garb, gear, manners and bottomless desires of their completed
Responsibilities; they are a shambles of a comic drill-team
But holy, holy—holy, becoming their own animate worshipful

Soon all but genderless flesh, a cooked sanctified recklessness—
O the old marks of elastic, leather, metal razors, callousing tools,
Pack straps and belts, fading from their embarrassed bodies!

THE CHANGES

Even at sea the bodies of the unborn and the dead
Interpenetrate at peculiar angles. In a displaced channel

The crew of a tanker float by high over the heads
Of a village of makers of flint knives, and a woman

In one round hut on a terrace dreams of her grandsons
Floating through the blue sky on a bubble of black oil

Calling her in the unknown rhythms of diesel engines to come
Lie down and couple. On the ship, three different sailors

Have a brief revery of dark, furry shanks, and one resolves
To build when he gets home a kind of round shrine or gazebo

In the small terraced garden of his house in a suburb.
In the garden, bees fumble at hydrangeas blue as crockery

While four children giggle playing School in the round gazebo.
(To one side, the invisible shaved heads of six priests

Bob above the garden's earth as they smear ash on their chests,
Trying to dance away a great epidemic; afterwards one priest,

The youngest, founds a new discipline based on the ideals
Of childlike humility and light-heartedness and learning.)

One of the sailor's children on his lunch hour years later
Writes on a napkin a poem about blue hydrangeas, bees

And a crockery pitcher. And though he is killed in a war
And the poem is burned up unread on a mass pyre with his body,

The separate molecules of the poem spread evenly over the globe
In a starlike precise pattern, as if a geometer had mapped it.

Overhead, passengers in planes cross and recross in the invisible
Ordained lanes of air traffic—some of us in the traverse

Passing through our own slightly changed former and future bodies,
Seated gliding along the black lines printed on colored maps

In the little pouches at every seat, the webs of routes bunched
To the shapes of beaks or arrowheads at the black dots of the cities.

THE LIVING

The living, the unfallen lords of life,
Move heavily through the dazzle
Where all things shift, glitter or swim—

As on a day at the beach, or under
The stark, absolute blue of a snow morning,
With concentric peals of brightness

Ringing in the cold air. They seem drugged.
Their abrupt good fortune clings heavily
With the slow sway and pomp of dirty velvet,

Their purple, the unaccustomed garb—
Worn slipshod—of the Court
Of Misrule: animal-headed, staring

As if sleepy or drunk, riding a goat
Or perched backwards on a donkey,
Widdershins, hectic. Beggars, bad governors,

We thrive awkwardly—some maimed slightly
In the course of war; some torn by fear sometimes;
Yet not paralyzed: we are moved. The strange

Stories of the degradations of the martyrs—
Crucified upside-down, cooked live
On a grille—bother us doubly: in themselves,

And because a strange opiate intervenes
As if they were suffering now, at this
Apex of time, and for some reason we

Could not concentrate, lost on the slopes
Below. We ape court manners clumsily;
Or shake fists, in awkward parade,

Exalated and confused. Even in affliction—grotesque
Illnesses, poverty, ruined hopes, the world's
Rage and the body's—the most miserable

Find in the mere daylight and air
A miraculous daily bread. Fairy bread:
We eat and are changed. Survivors

After a catastrophe, transported, feel
Nearly as if they could find the lost,
Luckless ones, somewhere, perhaps not far—

Crowded, maybe, behind some one
Of the innumerable doors of the palace.
Plump Chance beams like an effigy

Of Mardi Gras—the apparent origin
And end of so much: disease, fame,
Unemployment, intrigue. The world, random,

Is so real, it is as if our own
Good or bad luck were here only
As a kind of filler, holding together

Just that much of the adjacent
Splendor and terror. Only,
Sometimes, a sharp, violent burr, discordant,

Sizzles for one instant in jagged
Hachures in the brain—momentary scream
Of the powersaw wincing back

From a buried nail. Seizure: with a rising
Whoop, like a child on a steep slide,
A woman fell heavily to the floor

A few feet away from me, her scalp
Split a little, blood on my sleeve
As I raised her shoulders, acting the part

Of a stranger helping—asking a clerk
To please get something to cover her,
Please call for an ambulance, maybe

She has had a seizure. Epileptic—
The Falling Evil; something about the tongue,
Something for the teeth. But her mouth

Was not rigid, her eyes open—why
Should she look at me so knowingly,
Almost with contempt, was she crazy?—

As if I had made her fall: or were no
Stranger at all but a son, lover, lord
And master who had thus humiliated her

And now, tucking the blanket around her,
Hypocritical automaton, pretended
To urge—as if without complicity or shame

Or least sense of betrayal—the old embrace
Of this impenetrable haze, this prolonged
But not infinite surfeit of glory.

II

HISTORY OF MY HEART

One Christmastime Fats Waller in a fur coat
Rolled beaming from a taxicab with two pretty girls
Each at an arm as he led them in a thick downy snowfall

Across Thirty-fourth Street into the busy crowd
Shopping at Macy's: perfume, holly, snowflake displays.
Chimes rang for change. In Toys, where my mother worked

Over her school vacation, the crowd swelled and stood
Filling the aisles, whispered at the fringes, listening
To the sounds of the large, gorgeously dressed man,

His smile bemused and exalted, lips boom-booming a bold
Bass line as he improvised on an expensive, tinkly
Piano the size of a lady's jewel box or a wedding cake.

She put into my heart this scene from the romance of Joy,
Co-authored by her and the movies, like her others—
My father making the winning basket at the buzzer

And punching the enraged gambler who came onto the court—
The brilliant black and white of the movies, texture
Of wet snowy fur, the taxi's windshield, piano keys,

Reflections that slid over the thick brass baton
That worked the elevator. Happiness needs a setting:
Shepherds and shepherdesses in the grass, kids in a store,

The back room of Carly's parents' shop, record-player
And paper streamers twisted in two colors: what I felt
Dancing close one afternoon with a thin blond girl

Was my amazing good luck, the pleased erection
Stretching and stretching at the idea *She likes me,*
She likes it, the thought of legs under a woolen skirt,

To see eyes "melting" so I could think *This is it,*
They're melting! Mutual arousal of suddenly feeling
Desired: *This is it: "desire"!* When we came out

Into the street we saw it had begun, the firm flakes
Sticking, coating the tops of cars, melting on the wet
Black street that reflected storelights, soft

Separate crystals clinging intact on the nap of collar
And cuff, swarms of them stalling in the wind to plunge
Sideways and cluster in spangles on our hair and lashes,

Melting to a fresh glaze on the bloodwarm porcelain
Of our faces, Hey nonny-nonny boom-boom, the cold graceful
Manna, heartfelt, falling and gathering copious

As the air itself in the small-town main street
As it fell over my mother's imaginary and remembered
Macy's in New York years before I was even born,

II

And the little white piano, tinkling away like crazy—
My unconceived heart in a way waiting somewhere like
Wherever it goes in sleep. Later, my eyes opened

And I woke up glad to feel the sunlight warm
High up in the window, a brighter blue striping
Blue folds of curtain, and glad to hear the house

Was still sleeping. I didn't call, but climbed up
To balance my chest on the top rail, cheek
Pressed close where I had grooved the rail's varnish

With sets of double tooth-lines. Clinging
With both arms, I grunted, pulled one leg over
And stretched it as my weight started to slip down

With some panic till my toes found the bottom rail,
Then let my weight slide more till I was over—
Thrilled, half-scared, still hanging high up

With both hands from the spindles. Then lower
Slipping down until I could fall to the floor
With a thud but not hurt, and out, free in the house.

Then softly down the hall to the other bedroom
To push against the door; and when it came open
More light came in, opening out like a fan

So they woke up and laughed, as she lifted me
Up in between them under the dark red blanket,
We all three laughing there because I climbed out myself.

Earlier still, she held me curled in close
With everyone around saying my name, and hovering,
After my grandpa's cigarette burned me on the neck

As he held me up for the camera, and the pain buzzed
Scaring me because it twisted right inside me;
So when she took me and held me and I curled up, sucking,

It was as if she had put me back together again
So sweetly I was glad the hurt had torn me.
She wanted to have made the whole world up,

So that it could be hers to give. So she opened
A letter I wrote my sister, who was having trouble
Getting on with her, and read some things about herself

That made her go to the telephone and call me up:
"You shouldn't open other people's letters," I said
And she said "Yes—*who taught you that?*"

—As if she owned the copyright on good and bad,
Or having followed pain inside she owned her children
From the inside out, or made us when she named us,

III

Made me Robert. She took me with her to a print-shop
Where the man struck a slug: a five-inch strip of lead
With the twelve letters of my name, reversed,

Raised along one edge, that for her sake he made
For me, so I could take it home with me to keep
And hold the letters up close to a mirror

Or press their shapes into clay, or inked from a pad
Onto all kinds of paper surfaces, onto walls and shirts,
Lengthwise on a Band-Aid, or even on my own skin—

The little characters fading from my arm, the gift
Always ready to be used again. Gifts from the heart:
Her giving me her breast milk or my name, Waller

Showing off in a store, for free, giving them
A thrill as someone might give someone an erection,
For the thrill of it—or you come back salty from a swim:

Eighteen shucked fresh oysters and the cold bottle
Sweating in its ribbon, surprise, happy birthday!
So what if the giver also takes, is after something?

So what if with guile she strove to color
Everything she gave with herself, the lady's favor
A scarf or bit of sleeve of her favorite color

Fluttering on the horseman's bloodflecked armor
Just over the heart—how presume to forgive the breast
Or sudden jazz for becoming what we want? I want

Presents I can't picture until they come,
The generator flashlight Italo gave me one Christmas:
One squeeze and the gears visibly churning in the amber

Pistol-shaped handle hummed for half a minute
In my palm, the spare bulb in its chamber under my thumb,
Secret; or, the knife and basswood Ellen gave me to whittle.

And until the gift of desire, the heart is a titular,
Insane king who stares emptily at his counselors
For weeks, drools or babbles a little, as word spreads

In the taverns that he is dead, or an impostor. One day
A light concentrates in his eyes, he scowls, alert, and points
Without a word to one pass in the cold, grape-colored peaks—

Generals and courtiers groan, falling to work
With a frantic movement of farriers, cooks, builders,
The city thrown willing or unwilling like seed

(While the brain at the same time may be settling
Into the morning *Chronicle*, humming to itself,
Like a fat person eating M&Ms in the bathtub)

IV

Toward war, new forms of worship or migration.
I went out from my mother's kitchen, across the yard
Of the little two-family house, and into the Woods:

Guns, chevrons, swordplay, a scarf of sooty smoke
Rolled upwards from a little cratewood fire
Under the low tent of a Winesap fallen

With fingers rooting in the dirt, the old orchard
Smothered among the brush of wild cherry, sumac,
Sassafras and the stifling shade of oak

In the strip of overgrown terrain running
East from the train tracks to the ocean, woods
Of demarcation, where boys went like newly-converted

Christian kings with angels on helmet and breastplate,
Bent on blood or poaching. *There are a mountain and a woods*
Between us—a male covenant, longbows, headlocks. A pack

Of four stayed half-aware it was past dark
In a crude hut roasting meat stolen from the A&P
Until someone's annoyed father hailed us from the tracks

And scared us home to catch hell: We were worried,
Where have you been? In the Woods. With snakes and tramps.
An actual hobo knocked at our back door

One morning, declining food, to get hot water.
He shaved on our steps from an enamel basin with brush
And cut-throat razor, the gray hair on his chest

Armorial in the sunlight—then back to the woods,
And the otherlife of snakes, poison oak, boxcars.
Were the trees cleared first for the trains or the orchard?

Walking home by the street because it was dark,
That night, the smoke-smell in my clothes was like a bearskin.
Where the lone hunter and late bird have seen us

Pass and repass, the mountain and the woods seem
To stand darker than before—words of sexual nostalgia
In a song or poem seemed cloaked laments

For the woods when Indians made lodges from the skin
Of birch or deer. When the mysterious lighted room
Of a bus glided past in the mist, the faces

Passing me in the yellow light inside
Were a half-heard story or a song. And my heart
Moved, restless and empty as a scrap of something

Blowing in wide spirals on the wind carrying
The sound of breakers clearly to me through the pass
Between the blocks of houses. The horn of Roland

V

But what was it I was too young for? On moonless
Nights, water and sand are one shade of black,
And the creamy foam rising with moaning noises

Charges like a spectral army in a poem toward the bluffs
Before it subsides dreamily to gather again.
I thought of going down there to watch it a while,

Feeling as though it could turn me into fog,
Or that the wind would start to speak a language
And change me—as if I knocked where I saw a light

Burning in some certain misted window I passed,
A house or store or tap-room where the strangers inside
Would recognize me, locus of a new life like a woods

Or orchard that waxed and vanished into cloud
Like the moon, under a spell. Shrill flutes,
Oboes and cymbals of doom. My poor mother fell,

And after the accident loud noises and bright lights
Hurt her. And heights. She went down stairs backwards,
Sometimes with one arm on my small brother's shoulder.

Over the years, she got better. But I was lost in music;
The cold brazen bow of the saxophone, its weight
At thumb, neck and lip, came to a bloodwarm life

Like Italo's flashlight in the hand. In a white
Jacket and pants with a satin stripe I aspired
To the roughneck elegance of my Grandfather Dave.

Sometimes, playing in a bar or at a high school dance, I felt
My heart following after a capacious form,
Sexual and abstract, in the thunk, thrum,

Thrum, come-wallow and then a little screen
Of quicker notes goosing to a fifth higher, winging
To clang-whomp of a major seventh: listen to *me*

Listen to *me*, the heart says in reprise until sometimes
In the course of giving itself it flows out of itself
All the way across the air, in a music piercing

As the kids at the beach calling from the water *Look*,
Look at me, to their mothers, but out of itself, into
The listener the way feeling pretty or full of erotic revery

Makes the one who feels seem beautiful to the beholder
Witnessing the idea of the giving of desire—nothing more wanted
Than the little singing notes of wanting—the heart

Yearning further into giving itself into the air, breath
Strained into song emptying the golden bell it comes from,
The pure source poured altogether out and away.

III

RALEGH'S PRIZES

And Summer turns her head with its dark tangle
All the way toward us; and the trees are heavy,
With little sprays of limp green maple and linden
Adhering after a rainstorm to the sidewalk
Where yellow pollen dries in pools and runnels.

Along the oceanfront, pink neon at dusk:
The long, late dusk, a light wind from the water
Lifting a girl's hair forward against her cheek
And swaying a chain of bulbs.
                                        In luminous booths,
The bright, traditional wheel is on its ratchet,
And ticking gaily at its little pawl;
And the surf revolves; and passing cars and people,
Their brilliant colors—all strange and hopeful as Ralegh's
Trophies: the balsam, the prizes of untried virtue,
Bananas and armadillos that a Captain
Carries his Monarch from another world.

THE SAVING

Though the sky still was partly light
Over the campsite clearing
Where some men and boys sat eating
Gathered near their fire,
It was full dark in the trees,
With somewhere a night-hunter
Up and out already to pad
Unhurried after a spoor,
Pausing maybe to sniff
At the strange, lifeless aura
Of a dropped knife or a coin
Buried in the spongy duff.

Willful, hungry and impatient,
Nose damp in the sudden chill,
One of the smaller, scrawnier boys
Roasting a chunk of meat
Pulled it half-raw from the coals,
Bolted it whole from the skewer
Rubbery gristle and all,
And started to choke and strangle—
Gaping his helpless mouth,
Struggling to retch or to swallow
As he gestured, blacking out,
And felt his father lift him

And turning him upside down
Shake him and shake him by the heels,
Like a woman shaking a jar—
And the black world upside-down,
The upside-down fire and sky,
Vomited back his life,
And the wet little plug of flesh
Lay under him in the ashes.
Set back on his feet again

In the ring of faces and voices,
He drank the dark air in,
Snuffling and feeling foolish

In the fresh luxury of breath
And the brusque, flattering comfort
Of the communal laughter. Later,
Falling asleep under the stars,
He watched a gray wreath of smoke
Unfurling into the blackness;
And he thought of it as the shape
Of a newborn ghost, the benign
Ghost of his death, that had nearly
Happened: it coiled, as the wind rustled,
And he thought of it as a power,
His luck or his secret name.

THE QUESTIONS

What about the people who came to my father's office
For hearing aids and glasses—chatting with him sometimes

A few extra minutes while I swept up in the back,
Addressed packages, cleaned the machines; if he was busy

I might sell them batteries, or tend to their questions:
The tall overloud old man with a tilted, ironic smirk

To cover the gaps in his hearing; a woman who hummed one
Prolonged note constantly, we called her "the hummer"—how

Could her white fat husband (he looked like Rev. Peale)
Bear hearing it day and night? And others: a coquettish old lady

In a bandeau, a European. She worked for refugees who ran
Gift shops or booths on the boardwalk in the summer;

She must have lived in winter on Social Security. One man
Always greeted my father in Masonic gestures and codes.

Why do I want them to be treated tenderly by the world, now
Long after they must have slipped from it one way or another,

While I was dawdling through school at that moment—or driving,
Reading, talking to Ellen. Why this new superfluous caring?

I want for them not to have died in awful pain, friendless.
Though many of the living are starving, I still pray for these,

Dead, mostly anonymous (but Mr. Monk, Mrs. Rose Vogel)
And barely remembered: that they had a little extra, something

For pleasure, a good meal, a book or a decent television set.
Of whom do I pray this rubbery, low-class charity? I saw

An expert today, a nun—wearing a regular skirt and blouse,
But the hood or headdress navy and white around her plain

Probably Irish face, older than me by five or ten years.
The Post Office clerk told her he couldn't break a twenty

So she got change next door and came back to send her package.
As I came out she was driving off—with an air, it seemed to me,

Of annoying, demure good cheer, as if the reasonableness
Of change, mail, cars, clothes was a pleasure in itself: veiled

And dumb like the girls I thought enjoyed the rules too much
In grade school. She might have been a grade school teacher;

But she reminded me of being there, aside from that—as a name
And person there, a Mary or John who learns that the janitor

Is Mr. Woodhouse; the principal is Mr. Ringleven; the secretary
In the office is Mrs. Apostolacos; the bus driver is Ray.

A WOMAN

Thirty years ago: gulls keen in the blue,
Pigeons mumble on the sidewalk, and an old, fearful woman
Takes a child on a long walk, stopping at the market

To order a chicken, the child forming a sharp memory
Of sawdust, small curls of droppings, the imbecile
Panic of the chickens, their affronted glare.

They walk in the wind along the ocean: at first,
Past cold zinc railings and booths and arcades
Still shuttered in March; then, along high bluffs

In the sun, the coarse grass combed steadily
By a gusting wind that draws a line of tears
Toward the boy's temples as he looks downward,

At the loud combers booming over the jetties,
Rushing and in measured rhythm receding on the beach.
He leans over. Everything that the woman says is a warning,

Or a superstition; even the scant landmarks are like
Tokens of risk or rash judgment—drowning,
Sexual assault, fatal or crippling diseases:

The monotonous surf; wooden houses mostly boarded up;
Fishermen with heavy lines cast in the surf;
Bright tidal pools stirred to flashing

From among the jetties by the tireless salty wind.
She dreams frequently of horror and catastrophe—
Mourners, hospitals, and once, a whole family

Sitting in chairs in her own room, corpse-gray,
With throats cut; who were they? Vivid,
The awful lips of the wounds in the exposed necks,

Herself helpless in the dream, desperate,
At a loss what to do next, pots seething
And boiling over onto their burners, in her kitchen.

They have walked all the way out past the last bluffs,
As far as Port-Au-Peck—the name a misapprehension
Of something Indian that might mean "mouth"

Or "flat" or "bluefish," or all three: Ocean
On the right, and the brackish wide inlet
Of the river on the left; and in between,

Houses and landings and the one low road
With its ineffectual sea-wall of rocks
That the child walks, and that hurricanes

Send waves crashing over the top of, river
And ocean coming violently together
In a house-cracking exhilaration of water.

In Port-Au-Peck the old woman has a prescription filled,
And buys him a milk-shake. Pouring the last froth
From the steel shaker into his glass, he happens

To think about the previous Halloween:
Holding her hand, watching the parade
In his chaps, boots, guns and sombrero.

A hay-wagon of older children in cowboy gear
Trundled by, the strangers inviting him up
To ride along for the six blocks to the beach—

Her holding him back with both arms, crying herself,
Frightened at his force, and he vowing never,
Never to forgive her, not as long as he lived.

DYING

Nothing to be said about it, and everything—
The change of changes, closer or farther away:
The Golden Retriever next door, Gussie, is dead,

Like Sandy, the Cocker Spaniel from three doors down
Who died when I was small; and every day
Things that were in my memory fade and die.

Phrases die out: first, everyone forgets
What doornails are; then after certain decades
As a dead metaphor, *"dead as a doornail"* flickers

And fades away. But someone I know is dying—
And though one might say glibly, "everyone is,"
The different pace makes the difference absolute.

The tiny invisible spores in the air we breathe,
That settle harmlessly on our drinking water
And on our skin, happen to come together

With certain conditions on the forest floor,
Or even a shady corner of the lawn—
And overnight the fleshy, pale stalks gather,

The colorless growth without a leaf or flower;
And around the stalks, the summer grass keeps growing
With steady pressure, like the insistent whiskers

That grow between shaves on a face, the nails
Growing and dying from the toes and fingers
At their own humble pace, oblivious

As the nerveless moths, that live their night or two—
Though like a moth a bright soul keeps on beating,
Bored and impatient in the monster's mouth.

FLOWERS

The little bright yellow ones
In the January rain covering the earth
Of the whole bare orchard
Billions waving above the dense clumps
Of their foliage, wild linoleum of silly
Green and yellow. Gray bark dripping.

Or the formal white cones tree-shaped
Against the fans of dark leaf
Balanced as prettily in state
As the wife of the king of the underground
Come with palms on her hips to claim the golden apple of the sun.

Sexual parts; presents. Stylized to a central
O ringed by radiant lobes or to the wrapped
Secret of the rose. Even potatoes have them.
In his dead eyeholes
The clownish boy who drowned
In the tenth grade—Carl Reiman!—wears them
Lear wears them and my dead cousins
Stems tucked under the armpit
Buttons of orange in the mouth,

In a vernal jig they are propelled by them:
Dead bobbing in floral chains and crowns
Knee lifted by the pink and fuchsia
Half-weightless resurrection of heel and toe,
A spaceman rhumba. Furled white cup
Handfuls of violet on limp stems
The brittle green stalk held between arm and side
Of one certain dead poet—

And they push us away: when with aprons
Of petals cupped at our chin
We try to join the dance they put

Their cold hands on our chest
And push us away saying No
We don't want you here yet—No, you are not
Beautiful and finished like us.

THE GARDEN

Far back, in the most remote times with their fresh colors,
Already and without knowing it I must have begun to bring
Everyone into the shadowy garden—half-overgrown,

A kind of lush, institutional grounds—
Singly or in groups, into that green recess. Everything
Is muffled there; they walk over a rich mulch

Where I have conducted them together into summer shade
And go on bringing them, all arriving with no more commotion
Than the intermittent rustling of birds in the dense leaves,

Or birds' notes in chains or knots that embroider
The sleek sounds of water bulging over the dam's brim:
Midafternoon voices of chickadee, kingbird, catbird;

And the falls, hung in a cool, thick nearly motionless sheet
From the little green pond to shatter perpetually in mist
Over the streambed. And like statuary of dark metal

Or pale stone around the pond, the living and the dead,
Young and old, gather where they are brought: some nameless;
Some victims and some brazen conquerors; the shamed and the haunters;

The harrowed; the cherished; the banished—or mere background figures,
Old men from a bench, girl with glasses from school—all brought beyond
Even memory's noises and rages, here in the quiet garden.

A LONG BRANCH SONG

Some days in May, little stars
Winked all over the ocean. The blue
Barely changed all morning and afternoon:

The chimes of the bank's bronze clock;
The hoarse voice of Cookie, hawking
The Daily Record for thirty-five years.

SONG OF REASONS

Because of the change of key midway in "Come Back to Sorrento"
The little tune comes back higher, and everyone feels

A sad smile beginning. Also customary is the forgotten reason
Why the Dukes of Levis-Mirepoix are permitted to ride horseback

Into the Cathedral of Notre Dame. Their family is so old
They killed heretics in Languedoc seven centuries ago;

Yet they are somehow Jewish, and therefore the Dukes claim
Collateral descent from the family of the Virgin Mary.

And the people in magazines and on television are made
To look exactly the way they do for some reason, too:

Every angle of their furniture, every nuance of their doors
And the shapes of their eyebrows and shirts has its history

Or purpose arcane as the remote Jewishness of those far Dukes,
In the great half-crazy tune of the song of reasons.

A child has learned to read, and each morning before leaving
For school she likes to be helped through The Question Man

In the daily paper: Your Most Romantic Moment? Your Family Hero?
Your Worst Vacation? Your Favorite Ethnic Group?—and pictures

Of the five or six people, next to their answers. She likes it;
The exact forms of the ordinary each morning seem to show

An indomitable charm to her; even the names and occupations.
It is like a bedtime story in reverse, the unfabulous doorway

Of the day that she canters out into, businesslike as a dog
That trots down the street. The street: sunny pavement, plane trees,

The flow of cars that come guided by with a throaty music
Like the animal shapes that sing at the gates of sleep.

THE STREET

Streaked and fretted with effort, the thick
Vine of the world, red nervelets
Coiled at its tips.

All roads lead from it. All night
Wainwrights and upholsterers work finishing
The wheeled coffin

Of the dead favorite of the Emperor,
The child's corpse propped seated
On brocade, with yellow

Oiled curls, kohl on the stiff lids.
Slaves throw petals on the roadway
For the cortege, white

Languid flowers shooting from dark
Blisters on the vine, ramifying
Into streets. On mine,

Rockwell Avenue, it was embarrassing:
Trouble—fights, the police, sickness—
Seemed never to come

For anyone when they were fully dressed.
It was always underwear or dirty pyjamas,
Unseemly stretches

Of skin showing through a torn housecoat.
Once a stranger drove off in a car
With somebody's wife,

And he ran after them in his undershirt
And threw his shoe at the car. It bounced
Into the street

Harmlessly, and we carried it back to him;
But the man had too much dignity
To put it back on,

So he held it and stood crying in the street:
"He's breaking up my home," he said,
"The son of a bitch

Bastard is breaking up my home." The street
Rose undulant in pavement-breaking coils
And the man rode it,

Still holding his shoe and stiffly upright
Like a trick rider in the circus parade
That came down the street

Each August. As the powerful dragonlike
Hump swelled he rose cursing and ready
To throw his shoe—woven

Angular as a twig into the fabulous
Rug or brocade with crowns and camels,
Leopards and rosettes,

All riding the vegetable wave of the street
From the John Flock Mortuary Home
Down to the river.

It was a small place, and off the center,
But so much a place to itself, I felt
Like a young prince

Or aspirant squire. I knew that *Ivanhoe*
Was about race. The Saxons were Jews,
Or even Coloreds,

With their low-ceilinged, unbelievably
Sour-smelling houses down by the docks.
Everything was written

Or woven, ivory and pink and emerald—
Nothing was too ugly or petty or terrible
To be weighed in the immense

Silver scales of the dead: the looming
Balances set right onto the live, dangerous
Gray bark of the street.

AN EXPLANATION OF AMERICA

(1980)

LAIR

Inexhaustible, delicate, as if
Without source or medium, daylight
Undoes the mind; the infinite,

Empty actual is too bright,
Scattering to where the road
Whispers, through a mile of woods . . .

Later, how quiet the house is:
Dusk-like and refined,
The sweet Phoebe-note

Piercing from the trees;
The calm globe of the morning,
Things to read or to write

Ranged on a table; the brain
A dark, stubborn current that breathes
Blood, a deaf wadding,

The hands feeding it paper
And sensations of wood or metal
On its own terms. Trying to read

I persist a while, finish the recognition
By my breath of a dead giant's breath—
Stayed by the space of a rhythm,

Witnessing the blue gulf of the air.

An Explanation of America

A POEM TO MY DAUGHTER

PART ONE:
ITS MANY FRAGMENTS

I. Prologue: You

As though explaining the idea of dancing
Or the idea of some other thing
Which everyone has known a little about
Since they were children, which children learn themselves
With no explaining, but which children like
Sometimes to hear the explanations of,
I want to tell you something about our country,
Or my idea of it: explaining it
If not to you, to my idea of you.

Dancing is the expression by the body
Of how the soul and brain respond to music—
And yes, not only to the sensual, God-like,
Varying repetitions which we love
But also, I admit it, to harmony, too:
As of a group. But what the Brownies did
Gathered inside a church the other day
(Except for one flushed Leader, smiling and skipping
With shoes off through the dance) was Close Drill: frowning,
The children shuffled anxiously at command
Through the home-stitched formations of the Square Dance.
Chewing your nails, you couldn't get it straight.
Another Leader, with her face exalted
By something like a passion after order,
Was roughly steering by the shoulders, each
In turn, two victims: brilliant, incompetent you;
And a tight, humiliated blonde, her daughter.

But before going on about groups, leaders,
Churches and such, I think I want to try
To explain you. Countries and people of course
Cannot be known or told in final terms . . .
But can be, in the comic, halting way

Of parents, explained: as Death and Government are.
I don't mean merely to *pretend* to write
To you, yet don't mean either to pretend
To say only what you might want to hear.
I mean to write to my idea of you,
And not expecting you to read a word . . .
Though you are better at understanding words
Than most people I know. You understand
An Old Man's Winter Night. And I believe,
Compulsive explainer that I am, and you
Being who you are, that if I felt the need
To make some smart, professor-ish crack about
Walt Whitman, the Internment Camps, or *Playboy*
I could, if necessary, explain it to you,
Who, writing under the name of "Karen Owens,"
Began your "Essay on Kids": "*In my opinion,
We 'tots' are truly in the 'prime of life,'
Of all creatures on earth, or other planets
Should there be life on such.*"
                                        In games and plays,
You like to be the Bad Guy, Clown or Dragon,
Not Mother or The Princess. Your favorite creature
Is the Owl, the topic of another "Essay."
Garrulous, prosy, good at spelling and fond
Of punctuation, you cannot form two letters
Alike or on a line. You suck your thumb
And have other infantile traits, although
A student interviewing "tots" from five
To eight for her psychology project found,
Scaling results, that your ideas of God
And of your dreams were those of an adult.
Though I should never tell you that (or this)
It occurs to me, thinking of Chaplin, Twain
And others—thinking of owls, the sacred bird
Of Athens and Athene—that it is not
A type (the solitary flights at night;
The dreams mature, the spirit infantile)
Which America has always known to prize.
—Not that I mean to class you with the great
At your age, but that the celebrated examples
(Ted Williams comes to mind) recall your face,
The soft long lashes behind the owlish glasses
Which you selected over "cuter" frames:

That softness—feathery, protective, inward—
Muffling the quickness of the raptor's eye,
The gaze of liberty and independence
Uneasy in groups and making groups uneasy.

II. From the Surface

A country is the things it wants to see.
If so, some part of me, though I do not,
Must want to see these things—as if to say:

"I want to see the calf with two heads suckle;
I want to see the image of a woman
In rapid sequence of transparencies
Projected on a bright flat surface, conveying
The full illusion and effect of motion,
In vast, varying scale, with varying focus,
Swallow the image of her partner's penis.
I want to see enormous colored pictures
Of people with impossible complexions,
Dressed, often, in flamboyant clothes, along
The roads and fastened to the larger buildings.
I want to see men playing games with balls.
I want to see new cars; I want to see
Faces of people, famous, or in times
Of great emotion, or both; and above all,
It seems, I want to see the anthropomorphic
Animals drawn for children, as represented
By people in smiling masks and huge costumes.
I want to shake their hands. I want to see
Cars crashing; cards with a collie or a pipe
And slippers, dry flies, mallards and tennis rackets—
Two people kissing for Valentine, and then
A nicky-nacky design, a little puppy
Begging for me to like the person who mailed it."

In Mexico, I suppose they want to see
The Eyes of God, and dogs and ponies coupling
With women, skeletons in hats and skirts,
Dishwashers, plutocrats humiliated,
Clark Gable, flashy bauhaus buildings, pistols.
It always is disturbing, what a country
Of people want to see. . . . In England once,
A country that I like, between two Terms,
In Oxford, I saw a traveling carnival
And fair with Morris dancers, and a woman
Down in a shallow pit—bored-looking, with bored
And overfed, drugged-looking brown rats lolling

Around her white bare body where it was chained
Among them: sluggish, in a furtive tent.

And that was something, like the Morris dance,
Which an American would neither want
To see, nor think of hiding, which helps to prove
That after all these countries do exist,
All of us sensing what we want to see
Whether we want it separately, or not.

But beyond the kinds of ball or billboard, or what
The woman must undergo, are other proofs,
Suggesting that all countries are the same:
And that the awful, trivial, and atrocious
(Those "forms receptive, featureless and vast")
Are what all peoples want to see and hide,
Are similar everywhere, and every year
Take forms that are increasingly the same,
Time and *Der Spiegel*, Chile and Chicago,
All coming to one thing, whether sinister
Or bland as a Christmas card from "Unicef."

What do I want for you to see? I want—
Beyond the states and corporations, each
Hiding and showing after their kind the forms
Of their atrocities, beyond their power
For evil—the greater evil in ourselves,
And greater images more vast than *Time.*
I want for you to see the things I see
And more, Colonial Diners, Disney, films
Of concentration camps, the napalmed child
Trotting through famous newsfilm in her diaper
And tattered flaps of skin, *Deep Throat*, the rest.

I want our country like a common dream
To be between us in what we want to see—
Not that I want for you to have to see
Atrocity itself, or that its image
Is harmless. I mean the way we need to see
With shared, imperfect memory: the quiet
Of tourists shuffling with their different awes
Through well-kept Rushmore, Chiswick House, or Belsen;
"Lest we forget" and its half-forgotten aura.

I want for you to see a "hippie restaurant"
And the rock valley where a hundred settlers
Were massacred by other settlers, dressed
As Indians—like the Boston tea-tax rioters
Or like the college kids who work for Disney,
Showing the people what they want to see.

III. Local Politics

And so the things the country wants to see
Are like a nest made out of circumstance;
And when, as in the great old sermon "The Eagle
Stirreth Her Nest," God like a nesting eagle
Pulls out a little of the plush around us
And lets the thorns of trial, and the bramble,
Stick through and scrape and threaten the fledgling soul,
We see that that construction of thorn and bramble
Is like a cage: the tight and sheltering cage
Of Law and circumstance, scraping through the plush
Like death—whenever the eagle stirreth her nest,
The body with its bony cage of law
And politics, the thorn of death and taxes.

You, rich in rhetoric and indignation,
The jailbird-lawyer of the Hunnewell School,
Come home from some small, wicked parliament
To elaborate a new theme: forceful topics
Touching the sheeplike, piggish ways of that tyrant
And sycophantic lout, the Majority.
The two lame cheers for democracy that I
Borrow and try to pass to you ("It is
The worst of all the forms of government,
Except for all the others"—Winston Churchill)
You brush aside: Political Science bores you,
You prefer the truth, and with a Jesuit firmness
Return to your slogan: "Voting *is not* fair."

I have another saw that I can scrape
For you, out of the hoard of antique hardware,
Clichés and Great Ideas, quaintly-toothed
Black ironwork that we heap about our young:
Voting is one of the *"necessary evils."*
Avoid all groups and institutions, they
Are necessary evils: necessary
Unto the general Happiness and Safety,
And evil because they are deficient in being.
Such is the hardware; and somewhere in between
The avoidance and the evil necessity
We each conclude a contract with the Beast.

America is, as Malcolm X once said,
A prison. And that the world and all its parts
Are also prisons (Chile, the Hunnewell School,
One's own deficient being, each prison after
Its own degree and kind) does not diminish
Anything that he meant about his country:
When the Dan Ryan Expressway in Chicago
Was flooded, "Black youths" who the paper said
Pillaged the stranded motorists like beached whales
Were rioting prisoners . . . a weight of lead
Sealed in their hearts was lighter for some minutes
Amid the riot.
                    Living inside a prison,
Within its many other prisons, what
Should one aspire to be? a kind of chaplain?
But chaplains, I have heard, are often powers,
Political, within their prisons, patrons
And mediators between the frightened groups:
Blue People, Gray People, and their constricting fears,
The mutual circumstance of ward and warder.

No kind of chaplain ever will mediate
Among the conquering, crazed immigrants
Of El Camino and the Bergen Mall,
The Jews who dream up the cowboy films, the Blacks
Who dream the music, the people who dream the cars
And ways of voting, the Japanese and Basques
Each claiming a special sense of humor, as do
Armenian photo-engravers, and the people
Who dream the saws: *"You cannot let men live*
Like pigs, and make them freemen, it is not safe,"
The people who dream up the new diseases
For use in warfare, the people who design
New shapes of pants, and sandwiches sumptuous
Beyond the dreams of innocent Europe: crazed
As carpet-bombing or the Berlin Airlift—
Crazed immigrants and prisoners, rioting
Or else, alone as in the secrecy
Of a narrow bunk or cell, whittling or painting
Some desperate weapon or crude work of art:
A spoon honed to a dagger or a bauble,
A pistol molded from a cake of soap,
A fumbling poem or a lurid picture

Urgent and sentimental as a tattoo. . . .
The Dorians, too, were conquering immigrants,
And hemmed in by their own anarchic spirits
And new peninsula, they too resorted
To invented institutions, and the vote,
With a spirit nearly comic, and in fear.

The plural-headed Empire, manifold
Beyond my outrage or my admiration,
Is like a prison which I leave to you
(And like a shelter)—where the people vote,
And where the threats of riot and oppression
Inspire the inmates as they whittle, scribble,
Jockey for places in the choir, or smile
Passing out books on weekdays.
                                        On the radio,
The FM station that plays "All Country and Western"
Startled me, when I hit its button one day,
With a voice—inexplicable and earnest—
In Vietnamese or Chinese, lecturing
Or selling, or something someone wanted broadcast,
A paid political announcement, perhaps. . . .
"All politics is local politics"
Said Mayor Daley (in pentameter):
And this then is the locus where we vote,
Prisonyard fulcrum of knowledge, fear and work—
Nest where an Eagle balances and screams,
The wild bird with its hardware in its claws.

IV. Countries and Explanations

Gogol explains his country as a troika:
"What Russian doesn't like fast driving," he says,
"Exalted by the dark pines flashing past
Like smoke? . . . And you, my Russia—racing on
To God knows where in an endless, manic blur,
Like the most birdlike troika ever made
By a Russian peasant with an axe and chisel:
No screws, no metal—thundering past the milestones
Like spots before your eyes; and spreading out
Evenly over half the world! . . . A blur;
A jingling of bells, and rattling bridges; the road
Smokes under your wheels as everything falls behind;
The horses take fire, barely touching the earth;
And you become entirely a flow of air,
Inspired by God—Russia, where do you fly?"

She doesn't answer. The air is torn to shreds
And becomes mere wind behind the flying troika;
And the other countries, with nervous glances sideways—
So many pedestrians, startled at the curb—
Step to one side: astonished at the speed
And eloquence of Gogol's explanation,
His country thundering madly down the highway. . . .

Somebody might explain a troubled time
By saying, "It's because they killed the railroads":
Because a child who hears a whistle at night
Can hear it drawing closer to the bed
And further in a line, along a vein,
While highways murmuring in the night are like
A restless river, grown unpredictable
A way that rivers don't.
                              And yet the shadows
From headlights as they circled my bedroom walls
Have given me comfort too, the lights and whistle
Like two different sentimental songs
At night. And though the cars and highways do stifle
The downtowns and their sweet co-operation
(The City Bakery, the Paramount, the stores)
I love a car—a car, I guess, is like
One's personality, corrupt and selfish,

Full of hypnotic petty pains and joys,
While riding on a train is like the mind,
The separate reveries, the communal rhythm
Of motion in a line, along a vein. . . .

The communal speed of trains and happy freedom
In a car are like the troika: speed making plain
The great size of its place, the exhilaration
Of change which the size evokes—the schedules, pillows
And porters on the train, the thrill of wit
And aggression in a car, choosing a lane—
Yet someday, tamed and seasoned, our machines
Might make plain that America is a country:
Another country like others with their myths
Of their uniqueness, Tara and Golden Peru
And headlong Mother Russia or Colombia,
Finlandia and the Cowboy's Prayer, and even
Quiet Helvetia; each place a country
With myths and anthems and its heroic name.

And motion would be a place, and who knows, you
May live there in the famous national "love
Of speed" as though in some small town where children
Walk past their surnames in the churchyard, you
At home among the murmur of that place
Unthinkable for me, but for the children
Of that place comforting as an iceman's horse.

Because as all things have their explanations,
True or false, all can come to seem domestic.
The brick mills of New England on their rivers
Are *brooding, classic*; the Iron Horse is quaint,
Steel oildrums, musical; and the ugly suburban
"Villas" of London, Victorian Levittowns,
Have come to be civilized and urbane.

And so, although a famous wanderer
Defines a nation, "The same people living
In the same place," by such strange transformations
Of time the motion from place to place itself
May come to be the place we have in common.
The regions and their ways—like Northern Michigan
And its Rutabaga Pasties, or Union City

With its Cuban and Armenian churches—will be
As though Officially Protected Species.
The Shopping Center itself will be as precious
And quaint as is the threadmill now converted
Into a quaint and high-class shopping center.
For *place*, itself, is always a kind of motion,
A part of it artificial and preserved,
And a part born in a blur of loss and change—
All places in motion from where we thought they were,
Boston before it was Irish or Italian,
Harlem and Long Branch before we ever knew
That they were beautiful, and when they were:
Our nation, mellowing to another country
Of different people living in different places.

PART TWO:
ITS GREAT EMPTINESS

I. A Love of Death

Imagine a child from Virginia or New Hampshire
Alone on the prairie eighty years ago
Or more, one afternoon—the shaggy pelt
Of grasses, for the first time in that child's life,
Flowing for miles. Imagine the moving shadow
Of a cloud far off across that shadeless ocean,
The obliterating strangeness like a tide
That pulls or empties the bubble of the child's
Imaginary heart. No hills, no trees.

The child's heart lightens, tending like a bubble
Towards the currents of the grass and sky,
The pure potential of the clear blank spaces.

Or, imagine the child in a draw that holds a garden
Cupped from the limitless motion of the prairie,
Head resting against a pumpkin, in evening sun.
Ground-cherry bushes grow along the furrows,
The fruit red under its papery, moth-shaped sheath.
Grasshoppers tumble among the vines, as large
As dragons in the crumbs of pale dry earth.
The ground is warm to the child's cheek, and the wind
Is a humming sound in the grass above the draw,
Rippling the shadows of the red-green blades.
The bubble of the child's heart melts a little,
Because the quiet of that air and earth
Is like the shadow of a peaceful death—
Limitless and potential; a kind of space
Where one dissolves to become a part of something
Entire . . . whether of sun and air, or goodness
And knowledge, it does not matter to the child.

Dissolved among the particles of the garden
Or into the motion of the grass and air,
Imagine the child happy to be a thing.

Imagine, then, that on that same wide prairie
Some people are threshing in the terrible heat
With horses and machines, cutting bands
And shoveling amid the clatter of the threshers,
The chaff in prickly clouds and the naked sun
Burning as if it could set the chaff on fire.
Imagine that the people are Swedes or Germans,
Some of them resting pressed against the strawstacks,
Trying to get the meager shade.
                                        A man,
A tramp, comes laboring across the stubble
Like a mirage against that blank horizon,
Laboring in his torn shoes toward the tall
Mirage-like images of the tilted threshers
Clattering in the heat. Because the Swedes
Or Germans have no beer, or else because
They cannot speak his language properly,
Or for some reason one cannot imagine,
The man climbs up on a thresher and cuts bands
A minute or two, then waves to one of the people,
A young girl or a child, and jumps head-first
Into the sucking mouth of the machine,
Where he is wedged and beat and cut to pieces—
While the people shout and run in the clouds of chaff,
Like lost mirages on the pelt of prairie.

The obliterating strangeness and the spaces
Are as hard to imagine as the love of death . . .
Which is the love of an entire strangeness,
The contagious blankness of a quiet plain.
Imagine that a man, who had seen a prairie,
Should write a poem about a Dark or Shadow
That seemed to be both his, and the prairie's—as if
The shadow proved that he was not a man,
But something that lived in quiet, like the grass.
Imagine that the man who writes that poem,
Stunned by the loneliness of that wide pelt,
Should prove to himself that he was like a shadow
Or like an animal living in the dark.

In the dark proof he finds in his poem, the man
Might come to think of himself as the very prairie,
The sod itself, not lonely, and immune to death.

None of this happens precisely as I try
To imagine that it does, in the empty plains,
And yet it happens in the imagination
Of part of the country: not in any place
More than another, on the map, but rather
Like a place, where you and I have never been
And need to try to imagine—place like a prairie
Where immigrants, in the obliterating strangeness,
Thirst for the wide contagion of the shadow
Or prairie—where you and I, with our other ways,
More like the cities or the hills or trees,
Less like the clear blank spaces with their potential,
Are like strangers in a place we must imagine.

II. Bad Dreams

In a way, every stranger must imagine
The place where he finds himself—as shrewd Odysseus
Was able to imagine, as he wandered,
The ways and perils of a foreign place:
Making his goal, not knowing the real place,
But his survival, and his progress home.
And everyone has felt it—foreign ground,
With its demand on the imagination
Like the strange gaze of the cattle of the Sun—
Unless one is an angel, or a hick,
A tribesman who never made his wander-year.

People who must, like immigrants or nomads,
Live always in imaginary places
Think of some past or word to fill a blank—
The encampment at the Pole or at the Summit;
Comanches in Los Angeles; the Jews
Of Russia or Rumania, who lived
In Israel before it was a place or thought,
But a pure, memorized word which they knew better
Than their own hands.
                     And at the best such people,
However desperate, have a lightness of heart
That comes to the mind alert among its reasons,
A sense of the arbitrariness of the senses:
Blank snow subordinate to the textbook North.
Like tribesman living in a real place,
With their games, jokes or gossip, a love of skill
And commerce, they keep from loving the blank of death.

But there are perils in living always in vision—
Always inventing entire whatever paves
Or animates the innocent sand or snow
Of a mere locale. What if the place itself
Should seem a blank, as in a country huge
And open and potential? . . . the blank enlarges,
And swelling in concentric gusts of quiet
Absorbs the imagination in a cloud
Of quiet, as smoke disperses through a mist,
A vague chimera that engulfs the breath.

That quiet leads me to a stranger's dread
Of the place frightened settlers might invent:
The customs of the people there, the tongues
They speak, and what they have to drink, the things
That they imagine, might falter in such a place,
Or be too few; and men would live like Cyclopes,
"With neither assemblies nor any settled customs"—
Or Laestrygonians who consume their kind
And see a stranger as his meat and marrow,
And have no cities or cultivated farms.

A man who eats the lotus of his prairie
Or shadow—consumed by his desire for darkness
Till the mind seems itself a dreamy marrow—
Is like those creatures of a traveler's nightmare.
Even his sentiments about the deer,
Or grass, recall man-eating Polyphemus:
Who, when he cracks like a movie Nazi, sheds
Real tears, making a sentimental speech
To his pet ram.
     In place of settled customs,
Such a man might set up a brazen calf,
Or join a movement, fanatical, to spite
The spirit of assembly, or of words—
To drown that chatter and gossip, and become
Sure, like machines and animals and the earth.

Such a man—neither a Greek adventurer
With his pragmatic gods, nor an Indian,
Nor Jew—would worship, not an earth or past
Or word, but something immanent, like a shadow . . .
Perhaps he was once a Protestant, with a God
Whose hand was in every berry, insect, cloud:
Not in the Indian way, but as one hand,
Immanent, above that berry and its name.

And when that hand came to him as a prairie
He beheld pure space as if it were a god,
Or as a devil. And if he lost that hand,
Why wouldn't he—in his loneliness and love

Of thinking nothing—grow eager to lose himself
Among a brazen crowd, as in a calf,
A certain landscape, or a bird?
                                    Or say
That he sets out upon that empty plain
Immanent with a quiet beyond all thought
Or words, and that he settles on that ground
Of trial, to invent a mystic home—
And then discovers people there, engaged
Upon their commerce or their gossip, at home
Or wandering as in an actual place,
Attending to their ordinary business:
The ordinary passion to bring death
For gain or glory, as Odysseus
Might feel, would be augmented and inflamed
By the harsh passion of a settler; and so,
Why wouldn't he bring his death to Indians
Or Jews, or Greeks who stop for food and water,
To bustle and jabber on his tangled plain?

But my nightmare is not the one you have
To fear, exactly, and if the Cyclops comes
(Lumbering, hungry, unreasoning, drunk or blind)
He may come gently, without commotion, cloaked
More in the manner—as in poems by Auden—
Of a disquieting nurse, an official form
With its inquiry, than of my bad dreams.

For I am father and mother of my man
(Who is no man, but something I imagined,
Or a kind of word for something that I fear),
And perhaps I am his child, too: choosing to be
Myself explaining him, or him—like people
Who have mixed blood, and might feel free to choose
To be themselves as Indians, or Cowboys . . .
With their high cheekbones, blue eyes, and iron hair.

And you and I, who have no Indian blood
(Or Cowboy blood, assuming such a thing),
Imagine two sides of people—with their blood,
A place, a climate, their circumstances fixed
As bounds for choice or for imagination—
Hardly free: the takers ready to kill

To take the theater of their imagined home,
Still half imaginary; the defenders
At home in places that became the more
Imaginary as the white ones took
Tobacco; taught scalping; introduced the horse.

And even Malcolm X, who changed his name
So many times, whom we remember now
Most by that one name which still means "unknown"—
Possibly "free"—must, with his many names
And his red hair, have needed to consider
The kinds of arbitrariness and choice:
The arbitrariness of the blood and senses
Compared to the poles and summits of our choosing,
The textbook "Indian," "American" or "blood" . . .
The accumulating prison of the past
That pulls us towards a body and a place.

My imaginary man is in that prison,
Though he thinks only of the feral earth,
Making himself less free.
                              Then let him rest;
And think instead of the European poets
Posed thoughtfully with cigarettes or scarves,
As photographed for a fascist anthology
Of forty years ago, above their verses
About a landscape, tribe, or mystic shadow:
Caught in the prison of their country's earth
Or its Romantic potential, born of death
Or of a pure idea. " . . . *Italy*
(*Germany, Russia, America, Rumania*)
Had never really been a country," a book
Might say, explaining something.
                                    What I want
And want for you is not a mystic home
But something—if it must be imaginary—
Chosen from life, and useful. Nietzsche says
We should admire the traffickers and nomads

"Who have that freedom of the mind and soul
Which mankind learns from frequent changes of place,
Climate and customs, new neighbors and oppressors."

Americans, we choose to see ourselves
As here, yet not here yet—as if a Roman
In mid-Rome should inquire the way to Rome.
Like Jews or Indians, roving on the plains
Of places taken from us, or imagined,
We accumulate the customs, music, words
Of different climates, neighbors and oppressors,
Making encampment in the sand or snow.

III. Horace, Epistulae *I, xvi*

The poet Horace, writing to a friend
About his Sabine farm and other matters,
Implies his answer about aspiration
Within the prison of empire or republic:

"Dear Quinctius:
                    I'll tell you a little about
My farm—in case you ever happen to wonder
About the place: as, what I make in grain,
Or if I'm getting rich on olives, apples,
Timber or pasture.
                    There are hills, unbroken
Except for one soft valley, cut at an angle
That sweetens the climate, because it takes the sun
All morning on its right slope, until the left
Has its turn, warming as the sun drives past
All afternoon. You'd like it here: the plums
And low-bush berries are ripe; and where my cows
Fill up on acorns and ilex-berries a lush
Canopy of shade gives pleasure to their master.
The green is deep, so deep you'd say Tarentum
Had somehow nestled closer, to be near Rome.

There is a spring, fit for a famous river
(The Hebrus winds through Thrace no colder or purer),
Useful for healing stomach-aches and head-aches.
And here I keep myself, and the place keeps me—
A precious good, believe it, Quinctius—
In health and sweetness through September's heat.

You of course live in the way that is truly right,
If you've been careful to remain the man
That we all see in you. We here in Rome
Talk of you, always, as 'happy' . . . there is the fear,
Of course, that one might listen too much to others,
Think what they see, and strive to be that thing,
And lose by slow degrees that inward man
Others first noticed—as though, if over and over
Everyone tells you you're in marvelous health,
You might towards dinner-time, when a latent fever
Falls on you, try for a long while to disguise it,

1 8 1

Until the trembling rattles your food-smeared hands.
It's foolishness to camouflage our sores.

Take 'recognition'—what if someone writes
A speech about your service to your country,
Telling for your attentive ears the roll
Of all your victories by land or sea,
With choice quotations, dignified periods,
And skillful terms, all in the second person,
As in the citations for honorary degrees:
'Only a mind beyond our human powers
Could judge if your great love for Rome exceeds,
Or is exceeded by, Rome's need for you.'

—You'd find it thrilling, but inappropriate
For anyone alive, except Augustus.

And yet if someone calls me 'wise' or 'flawless'
Must one protest? I like to be told I'm right,
And brilliant, as much as any other man.
The trouble is, the people who give out
The recognition, compliments, degrees
Can take them back tomorrow, if they choose;
The committee or electorate decide
You can't sit in the Senate, or have the Prize—
'Sorry, but isn't that ours, that you nearly took?'
What can I do, but shuffle sadly off?
If the same people scream that I'm a crook
Who'd strangle my father for money to buy a drink,
Should I turn white with pain and humiliation?
If prizes and insults from outside have much power
To hurt or give joy, something is sick inside.

Who is 'the good man'?
                    Many people would answer,
'He is the man who never breaks the law
Or violates our codes. His judgment is sound.
He is the man whose word is as his bond.
If such a man agrees to be your witness,
Your case is won.'
                    And yet this very man,
If you ask his family, or the people who know him,
Is like a rotten egg in its flawless shell.

And if a slave or prisoner should say
'I never steal; I never try to escape,'
My answer is, 'You have your just rewards:
No beatings; no solitary; and your food.'

'I have not killed.' 'You won't be crucified.'
'But haven't I shown that I am good, and honest?'

To this, my country neighbor would shake his head
And sigh: 'Ah no! The wolf himself is wary
Because he fears the pit, as hawks the snare
Or pike the hook. Some folk hate vice for love
Of the good: you're merely afraid of guards and crosses.'

Apply that peasant wisdom to that 'good man'
Of forum and tribunal, who in the temple
Calls loudly on 'Father Janus' or 'Apollo'
But in an undertone implores, 'Laverna,
Goddess of thieves, O Fair One, grant me, please,
That I get away with it, let me pass as upright,
Cover my sins with darkness, my lies with clouds.'

When a man stoops to pluck at the coin some boys
Of Rome have soldered to the street, I think
That just then he is no more free than any
Prisoner, or slave; it seems that someone who wants
Too much to get things is also someone who fears,
And living in that fear cannot be free.
A man has thrown away his weapons, has quit
The struggle for virtue, who is always busy
Filling his wants, getting things, making hay—
Weaponless and defenseless as a captive.

When you have got a captive, you never kill him
If you can sell him for a slave; this man
Truly will make a good slave: persevering,
Ambitious, eager to please—as ploughman, or shepherd,
Or trader plying your goods at sea all winter,
Or helping to carry fodder at the farm. . . .
The truly good, and wise man has more courage;
And if need be, will find the freedom to say,
As in the *Bacchae* of Euripides:

King Pentheus, Lord of Thebes, what will you force me
To suffer at your hands?
                              I will take your goods.

You mean my cattle, furniture, cloth and plate?
Then you may have them.
                              I will put you, chained,
Into my prison, under a cruel guard.

Then God himself, the moment that I choose,
Will set me free. . . .

I think that what this means is: 'I will die.'

Death is the chalk-line towards which all things race."

IV. Filling the Blank

Odd, that the poet who seems so complacent
About his acorns and his cold pure water,
Writing from his retreat just out of Rome,
Should seem to end with a different love of death
From that of someone on a mystic plain—
But still, with love of death. " . . . A rather short man,"
He calls himself, "and prematurely gray,
Who liked to sit in the sun; a freedman's child
Who spread his wings too wide for that frail nest
And yet found favor, in both war and peace,
With powerful men. Tell them I lost my temper
Easily, but was easily appeased,
My book—and if they chance to ask my age
Say, I completed my forty-fourth December
In the first year that Lepidus was Consul."

I think that what the poet meant was this:
That freedom, even in a free Republic,
Rests ultimately on the right to die.
And though he's careful to say that Quinctius,
The public man able to act for good
And help his fellow-Romans, lives the life
That truly is the best, he's also careful
To separate their fortunes and their places,
And to appreciate his own: his health,
His cows and acorns and his healing spring,
His circle—"*We here in Rome*"—for friends and gossip.

It would be too complacent to build a nest
Between one's fatalism and one's pleasures—
With death at one side, a sweet farm at the other,
Keeping the thorns of government away. . . .

Horace's father, who had been a slave,
Engaged in some small business near Venusia;
And like a Jewish or Armenian merchant
Who does well in America, he sent
His son to Rome's best schools, and then to Athens
(It's hard to keep from thinking "as to Harvard")
To study, with the sons of gentlemen
And politicians, the higher arts most useful

To citizens of a Republic: math;
Philosophy; rhetoric in all its branches.

One March, when Horace, not quite twenty-one,
Was still at Athens, Julius Caesar died,
And the Roman world was split by civil war.

When Brutus came to Athens late that summer
On his way to Asia Minor—"half-mystical,
Wholly romantic Brutus"—Horace quit school
To follow Brutus to Asia, bearing the title
Or brevet-commission *tribunus militum,*
And served on the staff of the patriot-assassin.

Time passed; the father died; the property
And business were lost, or confiscated.
The son saw action at Philippi, where,
Along with other enthusiastic students
(Cicero's son among them), and tens of thousands
In the two largest armies of Roman soldiers
Ever to fight with one another, he shared
In the republican army's final rout
By Antony and Octavian.
                                Plutarch says
That Brutus, just before he killed himself,
Speaking in Greek to an old fellow-student,
Said that although he was angry for his country
He was deeply happy for himself—because
His virtue and his repute for virtue were founded
In a way none of the conquerors could hope,
For all their arms and riches, to emulate;
Nor could they hinder posterity from knowing,
And saying, that they were unjust and wicked men
Who had destroyed justice and the Republic,
Usurping a power to which they had no right.

The corpse of Brutus was found by Antony,
And he commanded the richest purple mantle
In his possession to be thrown over it,
And afterwards, the mantle being stolen,
He found the thief and had him put to death;
The ashes of Brutus he sent back to Rome,
To be received with honor by the mourners.

Horace came back to Rome a pardoned rebel
In his late twenties, without cash or prospects,
Having stretched out his wings too far beyond
The frail nest of his freedman father's hopes,
As he has written.
                    When he was thirty-five,
He published some poems which some people praised,
And so through Virgil he met the Roman knight
And good friend of Augustus, called Maecenas,
Who befriended him, and gave him the Sabine farm;
And in that place, and in the highest circles
In Rome itself, he spent his time, and wrote.

Since aspirations need not (some say, should not)
Be likely, should I wish for you to be
A hero, like Brutus—who at the finish-line
Declared himself to be a happy man?
Or is the right wish health, the just proportion
Of sun, the acorns and cold pure water, a nest
Out in the country and a place in Rome . . .

Of course, one's aspirations must depend
Upon the opportunities: the justice
That happens to be available; one's fortune.
I think that what the poet meant may be
Something like that; and as for aspiration,
Maybe our aspirations for ourselves
Ought to be different from the hopes we have
(Though there are warnings against too much hope)
When thinking of our children. And in fact
Our fantasies about the perfect life
Are different for ourselves and for our children,
Theirs being safer, less exciting, purer—
And so, depending always on the chances
Our country offers, it seems we should aspire,
For ourselves, to struggle actively to save
The Republic—or to be, if not like Brutus,
Like Quinctius: a citizen of affairs,
Free in the state and in the love of death . . .
While for our children we are bound to aspire
Differently: something like a nest or farm;
So that the cycle of different aspirations
Threads through posterity.

                    And who can say
What Brutus may come sweeping through your twenties—
Given the taste you have for noble speeches,
For causes lost and glamorous and just.

Did Horace's father, with his middle-class
And slavish aspirations, have it right?—
To give your child the education fit
For the upper classes: math, philosophy,
And rhetoric in all its branches; so I
Must want for you, when you must fall upon
The sword of government or mortality—
Since all of us, even you, race toward it—to have
The power to make your parting speech in Greek
(Or in the best equivalent) and if
You ever write for fame or money, that Virgil
Will pick your book out from a hundred others,
If that's not plucking at a soldered coin.

PART THREE:
ITS EVERLASTING POSSIBILITY

I. Braveries

Once, while a famous town lay torn and burning
A woman came to childbed, and lay in labor
While all around her people cursed and screamed
In desperation, and soldiers raged insanely—
So that the child came out, the story says,
In the loud center of every horror of war.
And looking on that scene, just halfway out,
The child retreated backward, to the womb:
And chose to make those quiet walls its urn.

"*Brave infant of Saguntum,*" a poet says—
As though to embrace a limit might show courage.
(Although the word is more like *bravo*, the glory
Of a great tenor, the swagger of new clothes:
The infant as a brilliant moral performer
Defying in its retreat the bounds of life.)

Denial of limit has been the pride, or failing,
Well-known to be shared by all this country's regions,
Races, and classes; which all seem to challenge
The idea of sufficiency itself . . .
And while it seems that in the name of limit
Some people are choosing to have fewer children,
Or none, that too can be a gesture of freedom—
A way to deny or brave the bounds of time.

A boundary is a limit. How can I
Describe for you the boundaries of this place
Where we were born: where Possibility spreads
And multiplies and exhausts itself in growing,
And opens yawning to swallow itself again?
What pictures are there for that limitless grace
Unrealized, those horizons ever dissolving?

A field house built of corrugated metal,
The frosted windows tilted open inward
In two lines high along the metal walls;
Inside, a horse-ring and a horse called Yankee
Jogging around the ring with clouds of dust
Rising and settling in the still, cold air
Behind the horse and rider as they course
Rhythmically through the bars of washed-out light
That fall in dim arcades all down the building.

The rider, a girl of seven or eight called Rose,
Concentrates firmly on her art, her body,
Her small, straight back and shoulders as they rise
Together with the alternate, gray shoulders
Of the unweary horse. Her father stands
And watches, in a business suit and coat,
Watching the child's face under the black serge helmet,
Her yellow hair that bounces at her nape
And part-way down her back. He feels the cold
Of the dry, sunless earth up through the soles
Of his thin, inappropriate dress shoes.

He feels the limit of that simple cold,
And braves it, concentrating on the progress
Of the child riding in circles around the ring.
She is so charming that he feels less mortal.
As from the bravery of a fancy suit,
He takes crude courage from the ancient meaning
Of the horse, as from a big car or a business:
He feels as if the world had fewer limits.
The primitive symbols of the horse and girl
Seem goods profound and infinite, as clear
As why the stuffs of merchants are called, "goods."

The goods of all the world seem possible
And clear in that brave spectacle, the rise
Up from the earth and onto the property
Of horses and the history of riding.

In his vague yearning, as he muses on goods
Lost and confused as chivalry, he might
Dream anything: as from the Cavalier
One might dream up the Rodeo, or the Ford,

Or some new thing the country waited for—
Some property, some consuming peasant dream
Of horses and walls; as though the Rodeo
And Ford were elegiac gestures; as though
Invented things gave birth to long-lost goods.

The country, boasting that it cannot see
The past, waits dreaming ever of the past,
Or all the plural pasts: the way a fetus
Dreams vaguely of heaven—waiting, and in its courage
Willing, not only to be born out into
The Actual (with its ambiguous goods),
But to retreat again and be born backward
Into the gallant walls of its potential,
Its sheltered circle . . . willing to leave behind,
It might be, carnage.
                              What shall we keep open—
Where shall we throw our courage, where retreat?

White settlers disembarked here, to embark
Upon a mountain-top of huge potential—
Which for the disembarking slaves was low:
A swamp, or valley of dry bones, where they lay
In labor with a brilliant, strange slave-culture—
All emigrants, ever disembarking. *Shall these*
Bones live? And in a jangle of confusion
And hunger, from the mountains to the valleys,
They rise; and breathe; and fall in the wind again.

II. Serpent Knowledge

In something you have written in school, you say
That snakes are born (or hatched) already knowing
Everything they will ever need to know—
Weazened and prematurely shrewd, like Merlin;
Something you read somewhere, I think, some textbook
Coy on the subject of the reptile brain.
(Perhaps the author half-remembered reading
About the Serpent of Experience
That changes manna to gall.) I don't believe it;
Even a snake's horizon must expand,
Inwardly, when an instinct is confirmed
By some new stage of life: to mate, kill, die.

Like angels, who have no genitals or place
Of national origin, however, snakes
Are not historical creatures; unlike chickens,
Who teach their chicks to scratch the dust for food—
Or people, who teach ours how to spell their names:
Not born already knowing all we need,
One generation differing from the next
In what it needs, and knows.
                            So what I know,
What you know, what your sister knows (approaching
The age you were when I began this poem)
All differ, like different overlapping stretches
Of the same highway: with different lacks, and visions.
The words—"*Vietnam*"—that I can't use in poems
Without the one word threatening to gape
And swallow and enclose the poem, for you
May grow more finite; able to be touched.

The actual highway—snake's-back where it seems
That any strange thing may be happening, now,
Somewhere along its endless length—once twisted
And straightened, and took us past a vivid place:
Brave in the isolation of its profile,
"Ten miles from nowhere" on the rolling range,
A family graveyard on an Indian mound
Or little elevation above the grassland. . . .

Fenced in against the sky's huge vault at dusk
By a waist-high iron fence with spear-head tips,
The grass around and over the mound like surf.

A mile more down the flat fast road, the homestead:
Regretted, vertical, and unadorned
As its white gravestones on their lonely mound—
Abandoned now, the paneless windows breathing
Easily in the wind, and no more need
For courage to survive the open range
With just the graveyard for a nearest neighbor;
The stones of Limit—comforting and depriving.

Elsewhere along the highway, other limits—
Hanging in shades of neon from dusk to dusk,
The signs of people who know how to take
Pleasure in places where it seems unlikely:
New kinds of places, the "overdeveloped" strips
With their arousing, vacant-minded jumble;
Or trashy lake-towns, and the tourist-pits
Where crimes unspeakably bizarre come true
To astonish countries older, or more savage . . .
As though the rapes and murders of the French
Or Indonesians were less inventive than ours,
Less goofy than those happenings that grow
Like air-plants—out of nothing, and alone.

They make us parents want to keep our children
Locked up, safe even from the daily papers
That keep the grisly record of that frontier
Where things unspeakable happen along the highways.

In today's paper, you see the teen-aged girl
From down the street; camping in Oregon
At the far point of a trip across the country,
Together with another girl her age,
They suffered and survived a random evil.
An unidentified, youngish man in jeans
Aimed his car off the highway, into the park
And at their tent (apparently at random)
And drove it over them once, and then again;
And then got out, and struck at them with a hatchet
Over and over, while they struggled; until

From fear, or for some other reason, or none,
He stopped; and got back into his car again
And drove off down the night-time highway. No rape,
No robbery, no "motive." Not even words,
Or any sound from him that they remember.
The girl still conscious, by crawling, reached the road
And even some way down it; where some people
Drove by and saw her, and brought them both to help,
So doctors could save them—barely marked.

                                       You see
Our neighbor's picture in the paper: smiling,
A pretty child with a kerchief on her head
Covering where the surgeons had to shave it.
You read the story, and in a peculiar tone—
Factual, not unfeeling, like two policemen—
Discuss it with your sister. You seem to feel
Comforted that it happened far away,
As in a crazy place, in *Oregon*:
For me, a place of wholesome reputation;
For you, a highway where strangers go amok,
As in the universal provincial myth
That sees, in every stranger, a mad attacker . . .
(And in one's victims, it may be, a stranger).

Strangers: the Foreign who, coupling with their cousins
Or with their livestock, or even with wild beasts,
Spawn children with tails, or claws and spotted fur,
Ugly—and though their daughters are beautiful
Seen dancing from the front, behind their backs
Or underneath their garments are the tails
Of reptiles, or teeth of bears.

                              So one might feel—
Thinking about the people who cross the mountains
And oceans of the earth with separate legends,
To die inside the squalor of sod huts,
Shanties, or tenements; and leave behind
Their legends, or the legend of themselves,
Broken and mended by the generations:
Their alien, orphaned, and disconsolate spooks,
Earth-trolls or Kallikaks or Snopes or golems,
Descended of Hessians, runaway slaves and Indians,
Legends confused and loose on the roads at night . . .
The Alien or Creature of the movies.

As people die, their monsters grow more tame;
So that the people who survived Saguntum,
Or in the towns that saw the Thirty Years' War,
Must have felt that the wash of blood and horror
Changed something, inside. Perhaps they came to see
The state or empire as a kind of Whale
Or Serpent, in whose body they must live—
Not that mere suffering could make us wiser,
Or nobler, but only older, and more ourselves. . . .

On television, I used to see, each week,
Americans descending in machines
With wasted bravery and blood; to spread
Pain and vast fires amid a foreign place,
Among the strangers to whom we were new—
Americans: a spook or golem, there.
I think it made our country older, forever.
I don't mean better or not better, but merely
As though a person should come to a certain place
And have his hair turn gray, that very night.

Someday, the War in Southeast Asia, somewhere—
Perhaps for you and people younger than you—
Will be the kind of history and pain
Saguntum is for me; but never tamed
Or "history" for me, I think. I think
That I may always feel as if I lived
In a time when the country aged itself:
More lonely together in our common strangeness . . .
As if we were a family, and some members
Had done an awful thing on a road at night,
And all of us had grown white hair, or tails:
And though the tails or white hair would afflict
Only that generation then alive
And of a certain age, regardless whether
They were the ones that did or planned the thing—
Or even heard about it—nevertheless
The members of that family ever after
Would bear some consequence or demarcation,
Forgotten maybe, taken for granted, a trait,
A new syllable buried in their name.

III. Mysteries of the Future

People stream slowly from a city church,
Their clothes bright in the sudden winter daylight,
Their bodies clean and warm inside the cloth
Like flags and armor in the dazzling air,
Sun flashing and wincing from the curbside ice.
Their pace is dreamy, strolling to their cars
Over the gritty sidewalk, in Sunday clothes.

It is Chicago; and though in many ways
It could be some place in another country,
The way I see the people and the church—
As mysteries, not just unknown or foreign—
Makes it this country: and Chicago, a setting
We make as we discover. It makes me think
Of how small children, with laborious
And grubby fingers, improvise a scene
From disproportionate, inspired arrangements
Of toys and objects: mirror for a pond,
And gathered on the shore amid strange buildings,
In mad, pedantic order, animals
And people. The squirrel, immense, bears on his shoulders
Riders including an anthropomorphic lion,
In pants and glasses. Barnyard and jungle creatures
Have landed their airplane—some are on the wings—
Right on the hotel roof. Wagons and cars
Parade down to the water. . . .
                                The girls and women
In pretty colors, the males in blue or brown,
Pause eddying on the steps, as though to blink
Like science-fiction travelers through time,
Uncertain if the surfaces they see
So brazenly gleaming mean to hail them toward
The mysteries of the past, or of the future.

Whether they have slept in church or not, they look
Refreshed in spirit, ready for the cuisine
And music of this era ahead or back,
Younger or older than the one they knew.

"For here we have no continuing city, but seek
For one to come"—*Hebrews* 13:14.

I can't say if our country is old, or young.
The future is an electrocuting thought—
That stuns the thinking reed to quiet, and heightens
The sense that everything we make is mortal,
Or part of some continuing epitaph.
Our very sentences are like a cloth
Cut shimmering from conventions of the dead—
Hung sometimes to flutter from a spar or gallant,
Nudged forward like the paper boats of candy
Launched for the gods downriver, in the future.

If I could sail forward to see the streets
Of that strange country where you will live past me,
Or further even by a hundred years;
And walk those pavements with my phantom steps,
And find Chicago flashing in winter sun;
And church doors ready to swing open, or melt
Before my penetrating ghost—my courage
Would fail, I think: best not to mount the steps
Where I could leave no footprint in the snow . . .
Best not to see those garments.
                              The shining casket,
Pure gold, where Philip of Macedonia lay
Twenty-three hundred years, and his breastplate
And greaves of gold and ivory, are gorgeous still;
But all the treasury of woven fabrics
And splendid leather that lay around the king
Technicians using instruments can deduce
Only from the fine dust scattered on the floor
Around the casket; the long hardwood handle
Of his bright spear fell slowly to a powder
Where it was propped, and left the point adhering
Eerily to the stonework of the wall.

It's fearful to leave anything behind,
To choose or make some one thing to survive
Into the future—where the air and light
That spread around us here in all directions
Stand ready to dim, discolor, and unravel
The colors that we fit around our bodies,
Precious and mutable, a second skin.

(Although the soul may be immortal, or not—
And some believe that even the body may rise—
Our cloth must die, and parch away forever.)

Jefferson in his epitaph records
That he was author of the Declaration
Of Independence, and of the Virginia law
Providing public education; and founder
Of that state's University—omitting
His "high office" . . . as if it were a bound,
Or something held, not something he had done—
The ceremonial garment he had been given
By others, with a certain solemn function
And honor; eventually, to be removed.

The church, Gothic Revival, and waiting cars
With brightwork glinting through a haze of salt
Suggest Nostalgia and Progress—which are in spirit
Less blatant, intimate, tragic than Epitaph:
As though the people, blood rising to their cheeks
As they walk into the cold, could leave behind
The image of themselves in their good clothes—
To survive as a memorial, compacted
By twenty centuries of the slowest fire
As if to something made of stone, or metal.

In the familiar boast or accusation
Americans have scant "historic sense";
Nostalgia and Progress seem to be our frail
National gestures against the enveloping,
Suffusive nightmare of time—which swallows first
The unaware, because they are least free . . .
But time's nightmare, and freedom from it, differ
For different peoples: like their burial customs;
And what they choose to say in what they leave.

To speak words few enough to fit a stone,
And frame them as if speaking from the past
Into the void or mystery of the future,
Demands that we be naked, free, and final:

God wills us free, man wills us slaves.
I will as God wills Gods will be done.
Here lies the body of
JOHN JACK
A native of Africa who died
MARCH 1773 aged about 60 years

Tho' born in a land of slavery,
He was born free,
Tho' he lived in a land of liberty,
He lived a slave,
Till by his honest, tho' stolen labors,
He acquired the source of slavery,
Which gave him his freedom,
Tho' not long before
Death the Grand Tyrant
Gave him his final emancipation,
And set him on a footing with kings.
Tho' a slave to vice,
He practiced those virtues
Without which kings are but slaves.

IV. Epilogue: Endings

"Pregnant again with the old twins, Hope and Fear" . . .
I'll write you one more time. You're older now,
By three years. And when the college students do
The Winter's Tale, you're charming as Mammilius,
The small bold Prince who starts what seems to be
A story about a ghost, and dies offstage
Before Act III is over—in time for bedtime,
Though you prefer to stay through each rehearsal,
As pleased as Puck, among the all-girl cast:
A kind of Court of Ladies, and you a page
Or favorite, a dwarf in jeans like theirs,
One of the group, all business, though inwardly
Half-drunk on glamour.
                           "Looking on the lines
Of my boy's face," the girl who plays your father
Pronounces, in lines you say from memory
As I drive you to rehearsal, "I did recoil
Twenty-three years, and saw myself unbreeched,
In my green velvet coat; my dagger muzzled,
Lest it should bite its master, and so prove,
As ornaments oft do, too dangerous."

Children are dangerous hostages to fortune—
Though they may seem, as to that fallible king,
Ornaments to our sentimental past,
They bind us to the future: Hope and Fear;
And though we might recoil, they make us strain
To see the wintry desert out beyond us.

On Opening Night, in hose and velvet tunic,
You say, *"a sad tale's best for winter"*—and yet,
The ending is happy; though the Bear eats the man,
Though the pastoral is broken, and the King alone
Upon the wind-scarred peak of his regret,
It all comes right: the statue comes to life,
And frozen Possibility moves and breathes,
Refreshed again, although the King is older.
Though happy endings rarely satisfy,
That one's a model of successful failure,
Holding Truth up against the rules of Romance.

The repetitious Phoenix, on her nest
Of burning contradictions, affronts belief
Like some impossible happy ending, as though
The country were just a dream—a pastoral
Delusion of the dirt and rocks and trees,
Or daydream of Leviathan himself,
A Romance of implausible rebirths.

The mountains intimate a different kind
Of ending: a cold and motionless remove.
High up above the treeline the clear dry air
Even in the warmest August noon conveys
A hint of snow; a crystal needle tickles
The nostrils a little, even while the eyes
Water and squint against the gray rock flashing,
The brightness of the sky.
                                    In the Sierras,
Where Winter's never far, the country is clear,
A stage of granite swept for meditation—
Irrelevant to the saunas, Volkswagens and woks
As British mountains are to tea and curry,
The exotic and assimilated clutter
Of treasure that expansion washed ashore.
Up there, a miner or drifter might expand
Upon his solitude and drift away
Over the ridges deep in muffling snow,
Feel free from all the clutter of hopes and fears,
And let his breath diffuse in the lucid cold.

Nothing can seem more final than the mountains,
Where Empires seem to grow and fade like moss—
But even mountains have come to need protection,
By special laws and organized committees,
From our ingenuities, optimism, needs.
The passion to make new beginnings can shatter
The highest solitude, or living rock. . . .

One might end with disgust for such renewals:
The old bear lumbers from the hibernation
Of all his crimes and losses; the new sunlight,
Resurgent, falls in a halo on his grizzle,
And he feels young again—*America*,

The air that serves me with the breath to speak . . .
In the "Minnesota Belt" from Times Square west
For five blocks, children, boy and girl blond hustlers
Imported from the Midwest, haunt all night—
Just as young children were sold in the Haymarket
Of William Morris's London, or the bazaars
Of ancient, drowsy Empires. But "It avails not,
Time nor place, distance avails not"; the country shrugs,
It is a cruel young profile from a coin,
Innocent and immortal in the religion
Of its own founding, and whatever happens
In actual New York, it is not final,
But a mere episode . . . and on some stage
As bare and rarefied as the coldest mountain,
With an authority transcending power
Or even belief, New Hope is born again,
And though it demand an Aztec vivisection
Everything lost must be made whole again.

A sad tale's best for winter, but the country
Sprawls over several zones of time and climate,
Never with any one season: the year itself
In no fixed place. Where nothing will stand still
Nothing can end—but recoils into the past,
Or is improvised into the dream or nightmare
Romance of new beginnings.
                                        On a lake
Beyond the fastness of a mountain pass
The Asian settlers built a dazzling city
Of terraced fountains and mosaic walls,
With rainbow-colored carp and garish birds
To adorn the public gardens. In the streets,
The artisans of feathers, bark or silk
Traded with trappers, with French and Spanish priests
And Scottish grocers. From the distant peaks,
The fabulous creatures of the past descended
To barter or to take wives: minotaur
And centaur clattered on the cobbled streets
With Norseman and Gypsy; from the ocean floor
The mermaid courtesans came to Baltimore,
New Orleans, Galveston, their gilded aquaria
Tended by powdered Blacks. Nothing was lost—
Or rather, nothing seemed to begin or end

In ways they could remember. The Founders made
A Union mystic yet rational, and sudden,
As if suckled by the very wolf of Rome . . .
Indentured paupers and criminals grew rich
Trading tobacco; molasses; cotton; and slaves
With names like horses, or from Scott or Plutarch.
In the mills, there was every kind of name,
With even "Yankee" a kind of *jankel* or Dutchman.
The Yankees pulled stones from the earth, to farm,
And when the glacial boulders were piled high,
Skilled masons came from Parma and Piacenza
And settled on Division Street and Oak Street
And on the narrow side streets between them. In winter,
Mr. Diehl hired Italian boys to help
Harvest the ice from Diehl's Pond onto sledges
And pack it into icehouses, where it kept
To be cut and delivered all summer long.

The Linden Apartments stand where Diehl's Pond was;
But even when I was little, the iceman came
To houses that had iceboxes, and we could beg
Splinters to suck, or maybe even a ride,
Sitting on wet floorboards and steaming tarps
As far as Saint Andrew's, or the V.F.W.
The Eagles, Elks, Moose, Masons each had a building:
I pictured them like illustrations from *Alice*.
As television came in, the lodges faded,
But people began to group together by hobbies,
Each hobby with its magazines and clubs;
My father still played baseball twice a week;
And even after you were born, the schools
And colleges were places set apart,
As of another time; and one time you
Performed in *The Winter's Tale*.
                              And at the end,
As people applauded louder and louder, you
Stood with young girls who wore gray wigs and beards,
All smiling and holding hands—as if the Tale
Had not been sad at all, or was all a dream,
And winter was elsewhere, howling on the mountains
Unthinkably old and huge and far away—
At the far opposite edge of our whole country,
So large, and strangely broken, and unforeseen.

MEMORIAL

(J.E. and N.M.S.)

Here lies a man. And here, a girl. They live
In the kind of artificial life we give

To birds or statues: imagining what they feel,
Or that like birds the dead each had one call,

Repeated, or a gesture that suspends
Their being in a forehead or the hands.

A man comes whistling from a house. The screen
Snaps shut behind him. Though there is no man

And no house, memory sends him to get tools
From a familiar shed, and so he strolls

Through summer shade to work on the family car.
He is my uncle, and fresh home from the war,

With little for me to remember him doing yet.
The clock of the cancer ticks in his body, or not,

Depending if it is there, or waits. The search
Of memory gains and fails like surf: the porch

And trim are painted cream, the shakes are stained.
The shadows could be painted (so little wind

Is blowing there) or stains on the crazy-paving
Of the front walk. . . . Or now, the shadows are moving:

Another house, unrelated; a woman says,
Is this your special boy, and the girl says, yes,

Moving her hand in mine. The clock in her, too—
As someone told me a month or two ago,

Months after it finally took her. A public building
Is where the house was: though a surf, unyielding

And sickly, seethes and eddies at the stones
Of the foundation. The dead are made of bronze,

But dying they were like birds with clocklike hearts—
Unthinkable, how much pain the tiny parts

Of even the smallest bird might yet contain.
We become larger than life in how much pain

Our bodies may encompass . . . all Titans in that,
Or heroic statues. Although there is no heat

Brimming in the fixed, memorial summer, the brows
Of lucid metal sweat a faint warm haze

As I try to think the pain I never saw.
Though there is no pain there, the small birds draw

Together in crowds above the houses—and cry
Over the surf: as if there were a day,

Memorial, marked on the calendar for dread
And pain and loss—although among the dead

Are no hurts, but only emblematic things;
No hospital beds, but a lifting of metal wings.

SADNESS AND HAPPINESS

(1975)

I. The Time of Year, The Time of Day

POEM ABOUT PEOPLE

The jaunty crop-haired graying
Women in grocery stores,
Their clothes boyish and neat,
New mittens or clean sneakers,

Clean hands, hips not bad still,
Buying ice cream, steaks, soda,
Fresh melons and soap—or the big
Balding young men in work shoes

And green work pants, beer belly
And white T-shirt, the porky walk
Back to the truck, polite; possible
To feel briefly like Jesus,

A gust of diffuse tenderness
Crossing the dark spaces
To where the dry self burrows
Or nests, something that stirs,

Watching the kinds of people
On the street for a while—
But how love falters and flags
When anyone's difficult eyes come

Into focus, terrible gaze of a unique
Soul, its need unlovable: my friend
In his divorced schoolteacher
Apartment, his own unsuspected

Paintings hung everywhere,
Which his wife kept in a closet—
Not, he says, that she wasn't
Perfectly right; or me, mis-hearing

My rock radio sing my self-pity:
"The Angels Wished Him Dead"—all
The hideous, sudden stare of self,
Soul showing through like the lizard

Ancestry showing in the frontal gaze
Of a robin busy on the lawn.
In the movies, when the sensitive
Young Jewish soldier nearly drowns

Trying to rescue the thrashing
Anti-semitic bully, swimming across
The river raked by nazi fire,
The awful part is the part truth:

Hate my whole kind, but me,
Love me for myself. The weather
Changes in the black of night,
And the dream-wind, bowling across

The sopping open spaces
Of roads, golf courses, parking lots,
Flails a commotion
In the dripping treetops,

Tries a half-rotten shingle
Or a down-hung branch, and we
All dream it, the dark wind crossing
The wide spaces between us.

THE TIME OF YEAR, THE TIME OF DAY

One way I need you, the way I come to need
Our custom of speech, or need this other custom
Of speech in lines, is to alleviate
The weather, the time of year, the time of day.

I mean for instance the way the dusk in late
Winter or early spring recalls adolescence:
The pity of my comical unease
And vague depression on the long walk home

From the grim school through washed-out extra daylight
And the yellow light that waited in kitchen windows,
Daydreaming victories on the long parades
Of artificial brick and bare hydrangea.

But how cold in retrospect the afternoon
And evening even in July could seem,
Cold heralding that now those very hours
Are on the way, the very hours which one

Had better use, which may be what it is
About the time of year and the time of day,
Their burden of a promise but a promise
Limited, that sends folk huddling to their bodies

Or kitchens as colonizers of the day
And of the year, rough settlers who throughout
The stunning winter couple in a fury
To fill the brown width of their tillable plains.

CEREMONY FOR ANY BEGINNING

Against weather, and the random
Harpies—mood, circumstance, the laws
Of biography, chance, physics—
The unseasonable soul holds forth,
Eager for form as a renowned
Pedant, the emperor's man of worth,
Hereditary arbiter of manners.

Soul, one's life is one's enemy.
As the small children learn, what happens
Takes over, and what you were goes away.
They learn it in sardonic soft
Comments of the weather, when it sharpens
The hard surfaces of daylight: light
Winds, vague in direction, like blades

Lavishing their brilliant strokes
All over a wrecked house,
The nude wallpaper and the brute
Intelligence of the torn pipes.
Therefore when you marry or build
Pray to be untrue to the plain
Dominance of your own weather, how it keeps

Going even in the woods when not
A soul is there, and how it implies
Always that separate, cold
Splendidness, uncouth and unkind—
On chilly, unclouded mornings,
Torrential sunlight and moist air,
Leafage and solid bark breathing the mist.

WAITING

When the trains go by
The frozen ground shivers
Inwardly like an anvil.

The sky reaches down
Stiffly into the spaces
Among houses and trees.

A wisp of harsh air snakes
Upward between glove
And cuff, quickening

The sense of the life
Elsewhere of things, the things
You touched, maybe, numb

Handle of a rake; stone
Of a peach; soiled
Band-Aid; book, pants

Or shirt that you touched
Once in a store . . . less
The significant fond junk

Of someone's garage, and less
The cinder out of your eye—
Still extant and floating

In Sweden or a bird's crop—
Than the things that you noticed
Or not, watching from a train:

The cold wide river of things,
Going by like the cold
Children who stood by the tracks

Holding for no reason sticks
Or other things, waiting
For no reason for the trains.

DECEMBER BLUES

At the bad time, nothing betrays outwardly the harsh findings,
The studies and hospital records. Carols play.

Sitting upright in the transit system, the widowlike women
Wait, hands folded in their laps, as monumental as bread.

In the shopping center lots, lights mounted on cold standards
Tower and stir, condensing the blue vapour

Of the stars; between the rows of cars people in coats walk
Bundling packages in their arms or holding the hands of children.

Across the highway, where a town thickens by the tracks
With stores open late and crèches in front of the churches,

Even in the bars a businesslike set of the face keeps off
The nostalgic pitfall of the carols, tugging. In bed,

How low and still the people lie, some awake, holding the carols
Consciously at bay, Oh Little Town, enveloped in unease.

DISCRETIONS OF ALCIBIADES

First frost is weeks off, but the prudent man
With house-plants on his front porch marks the season
And moves the potted *ficus* back indoors

While windows can be open for a while.
(The plant prefers a gradual transition.)
—The kid who did his homework, washed his face

And never wore tight pants, kept cherry bombs
And nasty photos in his briefcase (think:
A seventh-grader with a briefcase)—Hantman,

In Student Council with his red-hot bag:
His picture of a lady on all fours,
A Great Dane on her back, was not for sale.

And though he may have sold a bomb or two,
And must have set some off, I like to think
He preferred, like Presidents, their deep reserve.

Speaking of gradual transitions, "plant
Prefers" of course is only an expression.
You might say that the plant prefers to die,

Or wishes it were home, in Borneo,
Preferring never to have seen a window.
The stars are similar: "The wheeling Bear,

One white eye on the Pleiads, rolls another
At glowering Orion." Autumn stars.
On this first chilly dusk, a furry bat,

Warm-blooded, dips and flutters in the sky.
(Some constellations might be called, "The Bat.")
The roles are arbitrary too. The man

Who sleeps with Socrates and Leontes' wife,
Who knocks the cocks from his own effigies,
Or not, simply prefers—to use another

Expression—to hide his briefcase in a bomb.
Consider gods and heroes, how they merge:
(I speak as one believing in the gods,

Especially in quick, reflective Hermes,
So sensitive and practical—like a thief,
Or like long-suffering, shrewd Odysseus).

Apollo, sullen and glamorous obverse
Of Hermes, shrouds himself in dark, or shines,
Like bold Achilles in his tent—or out,

As he prefers. All one. Tithonus, too,
And Alcibiades, balling Lady Luck
Until she dried him up. When people say

"How was your summer?" who is there alive
Who wouldn't like to change sides, go to Sparta
Like Alcibiades, cut your hair, live clean . . .

And then knock up the king's wife on the sly.
That's where the inner briefcase is revealed:
He hoped his heir would be the King of Sparta—

More screwing with Fortuna, man with goddess . . .
From a god's point of view, it is perhaps
Disgusting, if exciting in a way,

Like a dog doing a lady from behind.
The sundry dogs from along the road prefer
To conduct ferocious gang-fucks in a field:

Dogs Only, in the end-of-summer fest.
But people, on Cape Cod, the Costa Brava,
Borneo, emulate gods and goddesses:

Rubbing their skin with oil, they sun it brown
Until they all are Spaniard, Jew or Greek—
Wear sandals; ply their boat; keep simple house

Cooking red meat or fish on open fires;
Market for salt; and dance to tinkly music.

TENNIS

TO HOWARD WILCOX

I. The Service

The nerve to make a high toss and the sense
Of when the ball is there; and then the nerve
To cock your arm back all the way, not rigid

But loose and ready all the way behind
So that the racket nearly or really touches
Your back far down; and all the time to see

The ball, the seams and letters on the ball
As it seems briefly at its highest point
To stop and hover—keeping these in mind,

The swing itself is easy; forgetting cancer,
Or panic learning how to swim or walk,
Forgetting what the score is, names of plants,

And your first piece of ass, you throw the racket
Easily through Brazil, coins, mathematics
And *haute cuisine* to press the ball from over

And a slight slice at two o'clock or less,
Enough to make it loop in accurately
As, like a fish in water flicking itself

Away, your mind takes up the next concern
With the arm, ball, racket still pressing down
And forward and across your obedient body.

II. Forehand

Straightforwardness can be a cruel test,
A kind of stagefright threatening on the cold
And level dais, a time of no excuses.

But think about the word *"stroke,"* how it means
What one does to a cat's back, what a brush
Does through a woman's long hair. Think about

The racket pressing, wiping, guiding the ball
As you stay on it, dragging say seven strings
Across the ball, the top edge leading off

To give it topspin. Think about the ball
As a loaf of bread, you hitting every slice.
Pull back the racket well behind you, drop it

And lift it, meeting the ball well out in front
At a point even with your left hip, stroking
To follow through cross-court. The tarnished coin

Of "follow through," the cat, the loaf of bread,
"Keep your eye on the ball," the dull alloy
Of homily, simile and coach's lore

As maddening, and as helpful, as the Fool
Or Æsop's *Fables*, the coinage of advice:
This is the metal that is never spent.

III. *Backhand*

Here, panic may be a problem; and in the clench
From back to jaw in panic you may come
Too close and struggling strike out with your arm,

Trying to make the arm do everything,
And failing as the legs and trunk resist.
All of your coinages, and your nerve, may fail . . .

What you need is the Uroborus, the serpent
Of energy and equilibrium,
Its tail between its jaws, the female circle

Which makes it easy: all is all, the left
Reflects the right, and if you change the grip
To keep your hand and wrist behind the racket

You suddenly find the swing is just the same
As forehand, except you hit it more in front
Because your arm now hangs in front of you

And not behind. You simply change the grip
And with a circular motion from the shoulder,
Hips, ankles, and knees, you sweep the inverted swing.

IV. *Strategy*

Hit to the weakness. All things being equal
Hit crosscourt rather than down the line, because
If you hit crosscourt back to him, then he

Can only hit back either towards you (crosscourt)
Or parallel to you (down the line), but never
Away from you, the way that you can hit

Away from him if he hits down the line.
Besides, the net is lowest in the middle,
The court itself is longest corner-to-corner,

So that a crosscourt stroke is the most secure,
And that should be your plan, the plan you need
For winning—though only when hitting from the baseline:

From closer up, hit straight ahead, to follow
The ball to net; and from the net hit shrewdly,
To get him into trouble so he will hit

An error, or a cripple you can kill.
If he gets you in trouble, hit a lob,
And make it towering to make it hard

For him to smash from overhead and easy
For you to have the time to range the backcourt,
Bouncing in rhythm like a dog or seal

Ready to catch an object in mid-air
And rocking its head—as with your plan in mind
You arrange yourself to lob it back, and win.

V. Winning

Call questionable balls his way, not yours;
You lose the point but have your concentration,
The grail of self-respect. Wear white. Mind losing.

Walk, never run, between points: it will save
Your breath, and hypnotize him, and he may think
That you are tired, until your terrible

Swift sword amazes him. By understanding
Your body, you will conquer your fatigue.
By understanding your desire to win

And all your other desires, you will conquer
Discouragement. And you will conquer distraction
By understanding the world, and all its parts.

II. Sadness And Happiness

SADNESS AND HAPPINESS

I

That they have no earthly measure
is well known—the surprise is
how often it becomes impossible
to tell one from the other in memory:

the sadness of past failures, the strangely
happy—doubtless corrupt—
fondling of them. Crude, empty
though the terms are, they do

organize life: sad American
house-hunting couples with kids
and small savings visit Model Homes
each Sunday for years; humble,

they need closet space, closet
space to organize life . . . in older
countries people seem to be happy
with less closet space. Empty space,

I suppose, also explains *post
coitum triste*, a phenomenon
which on reflection I am happy
to find rare in my memory—not,

II

God knows, that sex isn't crucial,
a desire to get more or better
must underlie the "pain" and "bliss"
of sonnets—or is it a need to *do* better:

A girl touched my sleeve, once,
held it, deep-eyed; life too at times
has come up, looked into my face,
My Lord, how like you this? And I?

Always distracted by some secret
movie camera or absurd audience
eager for clichés, *Ivanhoe*, de blues,
Young Man with A Horn, the star

tripping over his lance, quill, phallic
symbol or saxophone—miserable,
these absurd memories of failure
to see anything but oneself,

my pride, my consciousness, my shame, my
sickly haze of Romance—sick too
the root of joy? "Bale" and "bliss" merge
in a Petrarchist grin, that sleeve's burden

III

or chivalric trophy to bear as
emblem or mark of the holy
idiot: know ye, this natural stood
posing amiss while the best prizes

of life bounced off his vague
pate or streamed between his legs—
did Korsh, Old Russia's bedlam-sage,
enjoy having princesses visit his cell?

Would they dote on me as I shake out
a match, my fountain pen in the same
hand, freckling my dim brow with ink?
Into his muttered babble they read tips

on the market, court, marriage—I too
mutter: *Fool, fool!* or *Death!*
or *Joy!* Well, somewhere in the mind's mess
feelings are genuine, someone's

mad voice undistracted, clarity
maybe of motive and precise need
like an enamelled sky, cool
blue of Indian Summer, happiness

IV

like the sex-drowsy saxophones
rolling flatted thirds of the blues
over and over, rocking the dulcet
rhythms of regret, Black music

which tumbles loss over in the mouth
like a moist bone full of marrow;
the converse is a good mood grown
too rich, like dark water steeping

willow-roots in the shade, spotted
with sun and slight odor of dirt
or death, insane quibbles of self-
regard . . . better to mutter *fool*

or feel solaces of unmerited
Grace, like a road of inexplicable
dells, rises and lakes, found
in a flat place of no lakes—or feel

the senses: cheese, bread, tart
apples and wine, broiling acres
of sunflowers in Spain, mansards
in Vermont, painted shay and pard,

V

or the things I see, driving
with you: houses and cars, trees,
grasses and birds; people, incidents
of the senses—like women and men, dusk

on a golf course, waving clubs
dreamily in slow practice-gestures
profiled against a sky layered
purplish turquoise and gray, having

sport in the evening; or white
selvage of a mockingbird's gray
blur as he dabbles wings and tail
in a gutter—all in a way fraught,

full of emotion, and yet empty—
how can I say it?—all empty
of sadness and happiness, deep
blank passions, waiting like houses

and cars of a strange place,
a profound emptiness that came once
in the car, your cheekbone, lashes,
hair at my vision's edge, driving

VI

back from Vermont and then
into the iron dusk of Cambridge,
Central Square suddenly become
the most strange of places

as a Salvation Army band marches
down the middle, shouldering aside
the farting, evil-tempered traffic,
brass pitting its triplets and sixteenths

into the sundown fray of cops, gesturing
derelicts, young girls begging quarters,
shoppers and released secretaries, scruffy
workers and students, dropouts, children

whistling, gathering as the band
steps in place tootling and rumbling
in the square now, under an apocalypse
of green-and-pink sky, with paper

and filth spinning in the wind, crazy,
everyone—band, audience, city, lady
trumpeter fiddling spit-valve, John
Philip Sousa, me, Christianity, crazy

VII

and all empty except for you,
who look sometimes like a stranger;
as a favorite room, lake, picture
might look seen after years away,

your face at a new angle grows
unfamiliar and blank, love's face
perhaps, where I chose once to dream
again, but better, those past failures—

"Some lovely, glorious Nothing," Susan,
Patricia, Celia, forgive me—God,
a girl in my street was called Half-
A-Buck, not right in her head . . .

how happy I would be, or else
decently sad, with no past: you
only and no foolish ghosts
urging me to become some redeeming

Jewish-American Shakespeare
(or God knows what they expect,
Longfellow) and so excuse my thorny
egotism, my hard-ons of self-concern,

VIII

melodramas and speeches
of myself, crazy in love with
my status as a sad young man: dreams
of myself old, a vomit-stained

ex-Jazz-Immortal, collapsed
in a phlegmy Bowery doorway
on Old Mr. Boston lemon-flavored
gin or on cheap wine—that romantic

fantasy of my future bumhood
excused all manner of lies, fumbles,
destructions, even this minute, *"Mea
culpa!"* I want to scream, stealing

the podium to address the band,
the kids, the old ladies awaiting
buses, the glazed winos (who accomplished
my dream while I got you, and art,

and daughters): "Oh you city of
undone deathcrotches! Terrible
the film of green brainpus! Fog
of corruption at the great shitfry! No

IX

grease-trickling sink
of disorder in your depressed
avenues is more terrible
than these, and not your whole

aggregate of pollution
is more heavy than the measure
of unplumbed muttering
remorse, shame, inchoate pride

and nostalgia in any one
sulphur-choked, grit-breathing
citizen of the place. . . ." Sad,
the way one in part enjoys

air pollution, relishes
millennial doom, headlines,
even the troubles of friends—
or, OK, enjoys hearing

and talking about them, anyway—
to be whole-hearted is rare;
changing as the heart does, is it
the heart, or the sun emerging from

X

or going behind a cloud,
or a change somewhere in my eyes?
Terrible, to think that mere pretty
scenery—or less, the heraldic shape

of an oak leaf drifting down
curbside waters in the sun, pink
bittersweet among the few last
gray sad leaves of the fall—can bring

joy, or fail to. Shouldn't I vow
to seek only within myself
my only hire? Or not? All my senses,
like beacon's flame, counsel gratitude

for the two bright-faced girls
crossing the Square, beauty a light
or intelligence, no quarters for them,
long legs flashing bravely above

the grime—it is as if men were to
go forth plumed in white
uniforms and swords; how could we
ever aspire to such smartness,

XI

such happy grace? Pretty enough
plumage and all, a man in the bullshit
eloquence of his sad praises stumbles,
fumbles: *fool*. It is true, wonder

does indeed hinder love and hate,
and one can behold well with eyes
only what lies beneath him—
so that it takes more than eyes

to see well anything that is worth
loving; that is the sad part, the senses
are not visionary, they can tug
downward, even in pure joy—

trivial joy, the deep solid crack
of the bat. A sandlot home run
has led me to clown circling
the diamond as though cheered

by a make-believe audience
of thousands (you, dead poets, friends,
old coaches and teachers, everyone
I ever knew) cheering louder as I tip

XII

my imaginary, ironic hat and blow
false kisses crossing home, happiness
impure and oddly memorable as the sad
agony of recalled errors lived over

before sleep, poor throws awry
or the ball streaming through,
between my poor foolish legs, crouching
amazëd like a sot. Sport—woodmanship,

ball games, court games—has its cruel
finitude of skill, good-and-bad, as does
the bizarre art of words: confirmation
of a good word, *polvo*, dust, reddish gray

powder of the ballfield, *el polvo*
rising in pale puffs to glaze lightly
the brown ankles and brown bare feet in
Cervantes' poem of the girl dancing, all

dust now, poet, girl. It is intolerable
to think of my daughters, too, dust—
el polvo—or you whose invented game,
Sadness and Happiness, soothes them

XIII

to sleep: can you tell me one sad
thing that happened today, Can you think
of one happy thing to tell me that
happened to you today, organizing

life—not you too dust like the poets,
dancers, athletes, their dear skills
and the alleged glittering gaiety of
Art which, in my crabwise scribbling hand,

no less than Earth the change of all
changes breedeth, art and life
both inconstant mothers, in whose
fixed cold bosoms we lie fixed,

desperate to devise anything, any
sadness or happiness, only
to escape the clasped coffinworm
truth of eternal art or marmoreal

infinite nature, twin stiff
destined measures both manifested
by my shoes, coated with dust or dew which no
earthly measure will survive.

III. Persons

TO MY FATHER

FOR MILFORD S. PINSKY

The glazed surface of the world, dusk
And three mallard that land
In the dim lake, each

Scudding in a bright oval . . .
What chance, man, for the thin
Halting qualities of the soul?

Call this, prologue to an explanation,
Something like the way Uncle Joe Winograd
With a carpenter's flat silence

Might act on some given stretch
Of Uncle Italo Tarantola's lifelong
Lawyerly expanding monologue.

What I wanted, was to dwell
Here in the brain as though
At my bench, as though in a place

Like the live ongoing shop—
Between kitchen and factory—
Of a worker in wood or in leather:

Implements ranged in sizes and shapes,
The stuff itself stacked up
In the localized purposeful clutter

Of work, the place itself smelling
Of the hide, sawdust or whatever.
I wanted the exact words;

I wanted the way to pronounce
Evenly the judgment which a man
Who is quiet holds back as distinct

But not final in the presence
Of a good talker. I a good talker
Ask you a quiet man to recall the inside

Of a shop, glassdust and lenses
Everywhere, broken eyeglasses, forms
And odd pieces of paper, voices

Like phones ringing, tools
Broken and whole everywhere, mail
Unread, the sign—"Milford S." or

"Robert"—hanging like a straight face . . .
Surface, tyranny of the world visible,
Images that spread outward

From the brain like lines crazing—
Or like brief silvery ovals
That glide over the dark,

Ethereal, yet each wingbeat
Firm in time, of more
Substance than this, this mothlike

Stirring of words, work or affection.

OLD WOMAN

Not even in darkest August,
When the mysterious insects
Marry loudly in the black weeds
And the woodbine, limp after rain,
In the cooled night is more fragrant,
Do you gather in any slight
Harvest to yourself. Deep whispers
Of slight thunder, horizons off,
May break your thin sleep, but awake,
You cannot hear them. Harsh gleaner
Of children, grandchildren—remnants
Of nights now forever future—
Your dry, invisible shudder
Dies on this porch where, uninflamed,
You dread the oncoming seasons,
Repose in the electric night.

LIBRARY SCENE

TO P.S.

Under the ceiling of metal stamped like plaster
And below the ceiling fan, in the brown lustre

Someone is reading, in the sleepy room
Alert, her damp cheek balanced on one palm,

With knuckles loosely holding back the pages
Or fingers waiting lightly at their edges.

Her eyes are like the eyes of someone attending
To a fragile work, familiar and demanding—

Some work of delicate surfaces or threads.
Someone is reading the way a rare child reads,

A kind of changeling reading for love of reading,
For love and for the course of something leading

Her child's intelligent soul through its inflection:
A force, a kind of loving work or action.

Someone is reading in a deepening room
Where something happens, something that will come

To happen again, happening as many times
As she is reading in as many rooms.

What happens outside that calm like water braiding
Over green stones? The ones of little reading

Or who never read for love, are many places.
They are in the house of power, and many houses

Reading as they do, doing what they do.
Or it happens that they come, at times, to you

Because you are somehow someone that they need:
They come to you and you tell them how you read.

FIRST EARLY MORNINGS TOGETHER

Waking up over the candy store together
We hear birds waking up below the sill
And slowly recognize ourselves, the weather,
The time, and the birds that rustle there until

Down to the street as fog and quiet lift
The pigeons from the wrinkled awning flutter
To reconnoiter, mutter, stare and shift
Pecking by ones or twos the rainbowed gutter.

THE SENTENCES

Reading the sentences, November sun
Touching the avenues, offices, the station,
I saw you pass me on a street, your face
Was pink with cold, cold windows flashed, the stores
And cars were like—mythology—, the street
Itself was glamorous and lost, it was
As though I never knew you yet somehow knew
That this was you, a sentence interdicted
The present, it said, *you never knew*, you passed,
Leaves coppery and quick as lizards moved
Around your delicate ankles; November sun
Lay on the sidewalk, ordinary and final
As the sentences too flat for any poem.

DAUGHTER

I

She thinks about skeletons,
Admires their symmetry,
Responding with fear
To the implied movement
And the near-absence of expression.
In the museum
Of natural history
She pressed up close
To the smaller ones;
But shook, studying the tall
Scaffolding of dinosaurs
From the next room.
Back home, sitting in the john
With the door open
She claims to see, in a mirror
Down the dark hall, her own.

II

At certain times, midway
In a meal, or feeling
The dried mucus of her nose
She stares nowhere like a cat.
It is not quite the same
As the damp sensual trance
Of her thumb. It does not
Seem to be thought, nor
The deep stare of a cat
Concentrating on a noise
Or a smell. It is like a cat
Staring nowhere. When she comes
Out of it or is interrupted

A great emptiness flares,
Of profound privacy,
Like a good Christian's death.

III

With people, she deals oddly.
Normally too savage for bribes,
She attaches herself
In the way of a feudal tenant
To a grandma, overweight,
Spendthrift. The vassal
Declares prices,
Then haggles for a while.
She watches the two
Parents as they watch her
Pleasing herself with cheap
Toys and half-eaten sweets.
Chattering as two equals,
Nicole who calls herself "Mary"
And the woman nobody loves enough
Trot downtown for their perms.

IV

Like most children
She paints openly and well.
Somewhat like Henri Rousseau.
She and her friends paint
With a mild firmness
Of attention. Their great
Interest when they discuss
Paintings they have made
Seems partly affected:
A habit, maybe, grown
From the ineluctable
Deal that their kind make.
Is the painting also
Part of the deal? Often, she
Smears over her work, thick
Strokes, as for painting a wall.

V

She chats quietly
With a few cronies
On the subject of death.
They all have something to say,
Her contribution being
To list her close family
In correct order of age,
Declaring that we will die
In the same order. Nobody
Disagrees. *I know it,*
They say, *I know it.* One
Tells about graves. And then
They drift off the subject
Like that many businesslike
Starlings, flying away
From one tree among trees.

THE PERSONAL DEVIL

Ink, fire, quintuple mirrors—
By means bizarre enough,
I convoked the multiple eye
And saw from claw to scruff
The growth that Being nurtured:
The subtle bully whose Days—
His furies and lackeys and bearers—
Hang like the dozing flies
Whose billions in bog or orchard
Gorge with a daylong sigh.

The devices I arrayed
Conjured features like mine,
A familiar shape that I
Denied—denied as the bane
Of myself, the multifarious
Event that pulls my face
To its own. As I watched it fade
I saw myself take place,
Crystalline, in the iris
Of the huge, dissolving eye.

SPELUNKER

With flecks of web like foam
Still clinging to his brow and back
The deep explorer in his dream
Of rescue turns to seek

The faces of his friends
Already, as his arms come out
Into their cheering hands
Pulling him to the light

(Which thanks to certain drugs
Will not offend his eyes or skin)
And they will all be there; his legs
Will still be dangling down

Into the simple depth
(No symbol, no Womb or Self or Grave,
Neither his birth nor death
But a confusing cave

Where he is hurt and lost),
His feet still hanging in the dark
When to his mouth which they have kissed
The friends will hold a drink

Miraculously bright and cool,
The elixir of his dream,
His dream which marks the pall
Of darkness with cool stars for him,

Hallucinations which he knows
Are common in his plight
And which he now construes
As will-to-live, a faith in light

Surviving, so that he has come
To welcome this false Zodiac
Because it is his dream
Of rescue: for the sake

Of untrue lights to climb
Or burrow the expanding darkness
Which also is his dream
Of rescue, or the dream's dark likeness.

THE GENERATION BEFORE

TO FRANK BIDART

The wind blew. Some days, rain
Falling the size of nickels
Splashed up over the curb.
There were hats for that, and for sun
Too, frying shoeleather in its hot cycles.
Flesh was a poor garb,

So poor, the people were quaint—
Muffled up into their high cars
Or their quaint bulky clothing.
In the prolonged slap-happy Lent
Of the times, harder than yours,
Eating or asleep, breathing,

They got by in their manner, at times
Made Carnival in hotel bars,
At ball games or the track. In photographs,
In films, even in their haberdashery, games
And swank gear (cases, lighters,
Syphons, clips, objects for looks or laughs

Of glass, pigskin, malachite)
They survive as a vague murmur of style,
The nostalgic false life of a face
Shining from a snapshot. Time will not
Light gently on those fathers. They will fall
Sick in the lungs and the heart, hapless

In a motel, swearing at their own lost
Flickery past, craving a field
Empty and large, the growth pale and recent
Over the plow-twisting tangle of the past—
The grasses coarse, unculled,
The impossible field of the present.

IV. The Street Of Furthest Memory

THE STREET OF FURTHEST MEMORY

The street flails
old substances, a chaff
of felt, beaver-board,

slate shingles, tarpaper—plain
or made to resemble masonry
and brick—, oilcloth, sharkskin.

In a film of rain, the street
shines. Luncheonette,
lot, shoemaker,

They get clearer
in the rain, a spring rain
patched with sun,

the bright drops on glass,
on awnings of canvas, on cars
moving down the street

as the awnings flap,
flickering like a torn
film, coupe and sedan passing

to beyond your earliest
memory, on the street
out of memory, the sweet

street flailing its
lost substances, tangling
off as though thrown

from the spinning black
reel, unthreading rapidly, like
panic flailing the street.

LONG BRANCH, NEW JERSEY

Everything is regional,
And this is where I was born, dear,
And conceived,
And first moved to tears,
And last irritated to the same point.

It is bounded on three sides by similar places
And on one side by vast, uncouth houses
A glum boardwalk and,
As we say, The Beach.

I stand here now
At the corner of Third Avenue and Broadway
Waiting for you to come by in a car,
And count the red carlights
That rush through a fine rain
To where Broadway's two branches—North
Broadway and South Broadway—both reach
To the trite, salt, welcoming ocean.

DOCTOR FROLIC

Felicity the healer isn't young
And you don't look him up unless you need him.
Clown's eyes, Pope's nose, a mouth for dirty stories,
He made his bundle in the Great Depression

And now, a jovial immigrant success
In baggy pinstripes, he winks and wheezes gossip,
Village stories that could lift your hair
Or lance a boil; the small town dirt, the dope,

The fishy deals and incestuous combinations,
The husband and the wife of his wife's brother,
The hospital contract, the certificate . . .
A realist and hardy omnivore,

He strolls the jetties when the month is right
With a knife and lemons in his pocket, after
Live mussels from among the smelly rocks,
Preventative of impotence and goitre.

And as though the sight of tissue healing crooked
Pleased him, like the ocean's vaginal taste,
He'll stitch your thumb up so it shows for life.
And where he once was the only quack in town

We all have heard his half-lame joke, the one
About the operation that succeeded,
The tangy line that keeps that clever eye
So merry in the punchinello face.

PLEASURE PIER

With noises meaningful and vague as ever
The surf goes through its motions of attack.
Black water foams and comes erect and charges
White up the dark beach and collapses back to black.

Black under my feet, it sucks the kelp-haired pilings
That hold Convention Hall's Venetian folly
Up over the waters. The November air,
The boardwalk's void perspective, the melancholy

Of minarets and blistered stucco are blatant,
Crude as my crude vague needs, old hopes that dwell
On a violent urgency of color—blue mane
Of a horse frozen on the carousel,

A shooting-gallery bear whose eyes glare purple.
Among the sleeping pinballs and arcades
My boyhood lurks, as the phantom from a film
That the locale helps me dream. Hot-eyed, he wades

The boatride's oily channel, sleeps curled up
Among gears and pipes like viscera. In his arms
As he hurries through the tunnels of the Fun House
Is the Girl, the virgin whom he never harms.

Saved, she can't look when in the final scene
He dies in flames that throw their stagey lights
Out onto the water, the weary muttering waves
That pulled and worried at his prison's roots.

THE DESTRUCTION OF LONG BRANCH

When they came out with artificial turf
I went back home with a thousand miles.

I dug a trench by moonlight from the ocean
And let it wash in quietly

And make a brackish quicksand which the tide
Sluiced upward from the streets and ditches.

The downtown that the shopping centers killed,
The garden apartments, the garages,

The station, the Little Africa on (so help me)
Liberty Street, the nicer sections,

All settled gently in a drench of sand
And sunk with a minimum of noise.

The hollow of the shut-down movie house
Made bubbles. Wooden porches crumbled

But ranch homes in the new developments,
Tilting a little, slipped in whole.

I pushed back pieces that floated up: one gash
Of neon, the martini glass

That winked outside a mafia hotel;
A gas pump; a bouquet of socks

From Woolley's window (I even kept a few);
The pinball from my grandpa's bar.

I laid out hills and ridges, and with a brush
I creosoted lumps of sewage

Where the school had shat its plumbing as it went.
I fitted my carpet on the crust

(That made-in-Japan grass went on like magic)
With a neat margin at the beach,

And I still had half the night. "How great," I said . . .
Then, since forgiving had been fun

I thought I'd leave a monument or two.
Cautiously elegiac, I dug

Some scenes back up to compose my parkland vistas:
Benches and gloomy vegetation,

Some things already dead, an abandoned boardwalk,
Some weather, an unfilled foundation—

With a brush of huckleberry or a ragged fern,
Cabbagey growth along a curb,

Thin flags of sumac from a vacant lot
Avid in a tearing rain.

THE BEACH WOMEN

In the fierce peak of the day it's quietly they wade
With spread arms into the blue breakers rushing white
And swim seemingly with no tension, the arms
Curved, the head's gestures circular and slow.

They walk dripping back into the air
Of nineteen-fifty-five smiling downward from the glare
As if modestly, as they move daintily over the sand
Shaking their hair, tingling, taking it easy.

The beach flushes and broils, shapes ripple
In the waves of heat over it and the cold sea-water
Dries on their arms and legs and their suits, too,
Drying out stretched over their bottoms

In the luxury of sun flowering everywhere. The delicate
Salt glazing their skin they dissolve in oil.
Holiday colors throb on suits, towels, blankets,
Footwear, loose robes, bottles, carriers of straw,

Bright magazines and books, gear feminine and abundant
The whole overwhelming with a sense less of sex than gender,
The great oval blanks of their sunglasses hypnotic,
Flashing anonymous glamour over their cards, books or gossip.

It was Irving Stone they read, John O'Hara or Herman Wouk
Or the decade's muse of adultery: Grace Metalious.
With her picture in *Time*, floppy dungarees, no bra,
Retrospectively a seer, a social critic—

No doubt the cabana boys weren't always lying
About their own ladies, mistresses whose husbands
Came down from New York to tip big on the weekend—
Like Mrs. F, strawberry blond Italian . . .

What did she carry down to the sand all summer
But Wouk's *Caine Mutiny*, the earnest young sailors
Behaving like so many Jews, coming over guilty
Because they hadn't let Hitler as Lloyd Nolan

Played by Joe McCarthy send them under the waves.
Good for Grace, writing about "lust" with her flat
Characters and her big breasts. What did Mrs. F
Sunning at the shore fifteen years ago, or anyone,

Think about Caryl Chessman, Chaplin, Lucky Luciano,
Ike and the Rosenbergs? What can I recall? Women,
Moving in the sparkle of the sidewalk, blinding
Even in the reverse colors of the afterimage

Outside the drugstore where I worked, no cabana Lancelot,
Grateful for a wet cuddle with a chubby majorette.
I made club sandwiches and sundaes, on dark days purveyed
Dozens of copies of *Confidential*: "Victor Mature

Locked Me In A Cage" and "Russ Tamblyn's All Girl Party"
Cheered them up while the rain slashed gray
Soaking the boardwalk and gleaming on cars.
On those days I admired their tans, white dresses,

And pink oval fingernails on brown hands, and sold them
Perfume and lipstick, aspirins, throat lozenges and Tums,
Tampax, newspapers and paperback books—brave stays
Against boredom, discomfort, death and old age.

V. Essay on Psychiatrists

ESSAY ON PSYCHIATRISTS

I. *Invocation*

It's crazy to think one could describe them—
Calling on reason, fantasy, memory, eyes and ears—
As though they were all alike any more

Than sweeps, opticians, poets or masseurs.
Moreover, they are for more than one reason
Difficult to speak of seriously and freely,

And I have never (even this is difficult to say
Plainly, without foolishness or irony)
Consulted one for professional help, though it happens

Many or most of my friends have—and that,
Perhaps, is why it seems urgent to try to speak
Sensibly about them, about the psychiatrists.

II. *Some Terms*

"Shrink" is a misnomer. The religious
Analogy is all wrong, too, and the old,
Half-forgotten jokes about Viennese accents

And beards hardly apply to the good-looking woman
In boots and a knit dress, or the man
Seen buying the Sunday *Times* in mutton-chop

Whiskers and expensive running shoes.
In a way I suspect that even the terms "doctor"
And "therapist" are misnomers; the patient

Is not necessarily "sick." And one assumes
That no small part of the psychiatrist's
Role is just that: to point out misnomers.

III. *Proposition*

These are the first citizens of contingency.
Far from the doctrinaire past of the old ones,
They think in their prudent meditations

Not about ecstasy (the soul leaving the body)
Nor enthusiasm (the god entering one's person)
Nor even about sanity (which means

Health, an impossible perfection)
But ponder instead relative truth and the warm
Dusk of amelioration. The cautious

Young augurs with their family-life, good books
And records and foreign cars believe
In amelioration—in that, and in suffering.

IV. A *Lakeside Identification*

Yes, crazy to suppose one could describe them—
And yet, there was this incident: at the local beach
Clouds of professors and the husbands of professors

Swam, dabbled, or stood to talk with arms folded
Gazing at the lake . . . and one of the few townsfolk there,
With no faculty status—a matter-of-fact, competent,

Catholic woman of twenty-seven with five children
And a first-rate body—pointed her finger
At the back of one certain man and asked me,

"Is that guy a psychiatrist?" and by god he was! "Yes,"
She said, "He *looks* like a psychiatrist."
Grown quiet, I looked at his pink back, and thought.

V. *Physical Comparison With Professors And Others*

Pink and a bit soft-bodied, with a somewhat jazzy
Middle-class bathing suit and sandy sideburns, to me
He looked from the back like one more professor.

And from the front, too—the boyish, unformed carriage
Which foreigners always note in American men, combined
As in a professor with that liberal, quizzical,

Articulate gaze so unlike the more focused, more
Tolerant expression worn by a man of action (surgeon,
Salesman, athlete). On closer inspection was there,

Perhaps, a self-satisfied benign air, a too studied
Gentleness toward the child whose hand he held loosely?
Absurd to speculate; but then—the woman saw *something*.

VI. *Their Seriousness, With Further Comparisons*

In a certain sense, they are not serious.
That is, they are serious—useful, deeply helpful,
Concerned—only in the way that the pilots of huge

Planes, radiologists, and master mechanics can,
At their best, be serious. But however profound
The psychiatrists may be, they are not serious the way

A painter may be serious beyond pictures, or a businessman
May be serious beyond property and cash—or even
The way scholars and surgeons are serious, each rapt

In his work's final cause, contingent upon nothing:
Beyond work; persons; recoveries. And this is fitting:
Who would want to fly with a pilot who was *serious*

About getting to the destination safely? Terrifying idea—
That a pilot could over-extend, perhaps try to fly
Too well, or suffer from Pilot's Block; of course,

It may be that (just as they must not drink liquor
Before a flight) they undergo regular, required check-ups
With a psychiatrist, to prevent such things from happening.

VII. *Historical* (The Bacchae)

Madness itself, as an idea, leaves us confused—
Incredulous that it exists, or cruelly facetious,
Or stricken with a superstitious awe as if bound

By the lost cults of Trebizond and Pergamum . . .
The most profound study of madness is found
In the *Bacchae* of Euripides, so deeply disturbing

That in Cambridge, Massachusetts the players
Evaded some of the strongest unsettling material
By portraying poor sincere, fuddled, decent Pentheus

As a sort of fascistic bureaucrat—but it is Dionysus
Who holds rallies, instills exaltations of violence,
With his leopards and atavistic troops above law,

Reason and the good sense and reflective dignity
Of Pentheus—Pentheus, humiliated, addled, made to suffer
Atrocity as a minor jest of the smirking God.

When Bacchus's Chorus (who call him "most gentle"!) observe:
"Ten thousand men have ten thousand hopes; some fail,
Some come to fruit, but the happiest man is he

Who gathers the good of life day by day"—as though
Life itself were enough—does that mean, to leave ambition?
And is it a kind of therapy, or truth? Or both?

VIII. *A Question*

On the subject of madness the *Bacchae* seems,
On the whole, more *pro* than *contra*. The Chorus
Says of wine, "There is no other medicine for misery";

When the Queen in her ecstasy—or her enthusiasm?—
Tears her terrified son's arm from his body, or bears
His head on her spear, she remains happy so long

As she remains crazy; the God himself (who bound fawnskin
To the women's flesh, armed them with ivy arrows
And his orgies' livery) debases poor Pentheus first,

Then leads him to mince capering towards female Death
And dismemberment: flushed, grinning, the grave young
King of Thebes pulls at a slipping bra-strap, simpers

Down at his turned ankle. *Pentheus*: "Should I lift up
Mount Cithæron—Bacchae, mother and all?"
Dionysus: "Do what you want to do. Your mind

Was unstable once, but now you sound more sane,
You are on your way to great things." The question is,
Which is the psychiatrist: Pentheus, or Dionysus?

IX. Pentheus As Psychiatrist

With his reasonable questions Pentheus tries
To throw light on the old customs of savagery.
Like a brave doctor, he asks about it all,

He hears everything, "Weird, fantastic things"
The Messenger calls them: with their breasts
Swollen, their new babies abandoned, mothers

Among the Bacchantes nestled gazelles
And young wolves in their arms, and suckled them;
You might see a single one of them tear a fat calf

In two, still bellowing with fright, while others
Clawed heifers to pieces; ribs and hooves
Were strewn everywhere; blood-smeared scraps

Hung from the fir trees; furious bulls
Charged and then fell stumbling, pulled down
To be stripped of skin and flesh by screaming women . . .

And Pentheus listened. Flames burned in their hair,
Unnoticed; thick honey spurted from their wands;
And the snakes they wore like ribbons licked

Hot blood from their flushed necks: Pentheus
Was the man the people told . . . "weird things," like
A middle-class fantasy of release; and when even

The old men—bent Cadmus and Tiresias—dress up
In fawnskin and ivy, beating their wands on the ground,
Trying to carouse, it is Pentheus—down-to-earth,

Sober—who raises his voice in the name of dignity.
Being a psychiatrist, how could he attend to the Chorus's warning
Against "those who aspire" and "a tongue without reins"?

X. *Dionysus As Psychiatrist*

In a more hostile view, the psychiatrists
Are like Bacchus—the knowing smirk of his mask,
His patients, his confident guidance of passion,

And even his little jokes, as when the great palace
Is hit by lightning which blazes and stays,
Bouncing among the crumpled stone walls . . .

And through the burning rubble he comes,
With his soft ways picking along lightly
With a calm smile for the trembling Chorus

Who have fallen to the ground, bowing
In the un-Greek, Eastern way—What, Asian women,
He asks, Were you disturbed just now when Bacchus

Jostled the palace? He warns Pentheus to adjust,
To learn the ordinary man's humble sense of limits,
Violent limits, to the rational world. He cures

Pentheus of the grand delusion that the dark
Urgencies can be governed simply by the mind,
And the mind's will. He teaches Queen Agave to look

Up from her loom, up at the light, at her tall
Son's head impaled on the stiff spear clutched
In her own hand soiled with dirt and blood.

XI. *Their Philistinism Considered*

"Greek Tragedy" of course is the sort of thing
They like and like the idea of . . . though not "tragedy"
In the sense of newspapers. When a patient shot one of them,

People phoned in, many upset as though a deep,
Special rule had been abrogated, someone had gone too far.
The poor doctor, as described by the evening *Globe*,

Turned out to be a decent, conventional man (Doctors
For Peace, B'Nai Brith, numerous articles), almost
Carefully so, like Paul Valéry—or like Rex Morgan, M.D., who,

In the same *Globe*, attends a concert with a longjawed woman.
First Panel: *"We're a little early for the concert!*
There's an art museum we can stroll through!" *"I'd like*

That, Dr. Morgan!" Second Panel: *"Outside the hospital,*
There's no need for such formality, Karen! Call me
By my first name!" *"I'll feel a little awkward!"*

Final Panel: *"Meanwhile . . ."* a black car pulls up
To City Hospital. . . . By the next day's *Globe*, the real
Doctor has died of gunshot wounds, while for smiling, wooden,

Masklike Rex and his companion the concert has passed,
Painlessly, offstage: *"This was a beautiful experience, Rex!"*
"I'm glad you enjoyed it! I have season tickets

And you're welcome to use them! I don't have
The opportunity to go to many of the concerts!"
Second Panel: *"You must be famished!"* And so Rex

And Karen go off to smile over a meal which will pass
Like music offstage, off to the mysterious pathos
Of their exclamation marks, while in the final panel

"Meanwhile, In The Lobby At City Hospital"
A longjawed man paces furiously among
The lamps, magazines, tables and tubular chairs.

XII. Their Philistinism Dismissed

But after all—what "cultural life" and what
Furniture, what set of the face, would seem adequate
For those who supply medicine for misery?

After all, what they do is in a way a kind of art,
And what writers have to say about music, or painters'
Views about poetry, musicians' taste in pictures, all

Often are similarly hoked-up, dutiful, vulgar. After all,
They are not gods or heroes, nor even priests chosen
Apart from their own powers, but like artists are mere

Experts dependent on their own wisdom, their own arts:
Pilgrims in the world, journeymen, bourgeois savants,
Gallant seekers and persistent sons, doomed

To their cruel furniture and their season tickets
As to skimped meditations and waxen odes.
At first, Rex Morgan seems a perfect Pentheus—

But he smirks, he is imperturbable, he understates;
Understatement is the privilege of a god, we must
Choose, we must find out which way to see them:

Either the bland arrogance of the abrupt mountain god
Or the man of the town doing his best, we must not
Complain both that they are inhuman and too human.

XIII. *Their Despair*

I am quite sure that I have read somewhere
That the rate of suicide among psychiatrists
Is far higher than for any other profession.

There are many myths to explain such things, things
Which one reads and believes without believing
Any one significance for them—as in this case,

Which again reminds me of writers, who, I have read,
Drink and become alcoholics and die of alcoholism
In far greater numbers than other people.

Symmetry suggests one myth, or significance: the drinking
Of writers coming from too much concentration,
In solitude, upon feelings expressed

For or even about possibly indifferent people, people
Who are absent or perhaps dead, or unborn; the suicide
Of psychiatrists coming from too much attention,

In most intimate contact, concentrated upon the feelings
Of people toward whom one may feel indifferent,
People who are certain, sooner or later, to die . . .

Or people about whom they care too much, after all?
The significance of any life, of its misery and its end,
Is not absolute—that is the despair which

Underlies their good sense, recycling their garbage,
Voting, attending town-meetings, synagogues, churches,
Weddings, contingent gatherings of all kinds.

XIV. Their Speech, Compared With Wisdom And Poetry

Terms of all kinds mellow with time, growing
Arbitrary and rich as we call this man "neurotic"
Or that man "a peacock." The lore of psychiatrists—

"Paranoid," "Anal" and so on, if they still use
Such terms—also passes into the status of old sayings:
Water thinner than blood or under bridges; bridges

Crossed in the future or burnt in the past. Or the terms
Of myth, the phrases that well up in my mind:
Two blind women and a blind little boy, running—

Easier to cut thin air into planks with a saw
And then drive nails into those planks of air,
Than to evade those three, the blind harriers,

The tireless blind women and the blind boy, pursuing
For long years of my life, for long centuries of time.
Concerning Justice, Fortune and Love I believe

That there may be wisdom, but no science and few terms:
Blind, and blinding, too. Hot in pursuit and flight,
Justice, Fortune and Love demand the arts

Of knowing and naming: and, yes, the psychiatrists, too,
Patiently naming them. But all in pursuit and flight, two
Blind women, tireless, and the blind little boy.

XV. A *Footnote Concerning Psychiatry Itself*

Having mentioned it, though it is not
My subject here, I will say only that one
Hopes it is good, and hopes that practicing it

The psychiatrists who are my subject here
Will respect the means, however pathetic,
That precede them; that they respect the patient's

Own previous efforts, strategies, civilizations—
Not only whatever it is that lets a man consciously
Desire girls of sixteen (or less) on the street,

And not embrace them, et cetera, but everything that was
There already: the restraints, and the other lawful
Old culture of wine, women, et cetera.

XVI. *Generalizing, Just And Unjust*

As far as one can generalize, only a few
Are not Jewish. Many, I have heard, grew up
As an only child. Among many general charges

Brought against them (smugness, obfuscation)
Is a hard, venal quality. In truth, they do differ
From most people in the special, tax-deductible status

Of their services, an enviable privilege which brings
Venality to the eye of the beholder, who feels
With some justice that if to soothe misery

Is a tax-deductible medical cost, then the lute-player,
Waitress, and actor also deserve to offer
Their services as tax-deductible; movies and TV

Should be tax-deductible . . . or nothing should;
Such cash matters perhaps lead psychiatrists
And others to buy what ought not to be sold: Seder

Services at hotels; skill at games from paid lessons;
Fast divorce; the winning side in a war seen
On TV like cowboys or football—*that* is how much

One can generalize: psychiatrists are as alike (and unlike)
As cowboys. In fact, they are stock characters like cowboys:
"Bette Davis, Claude Rains in *Now, Voyager* (1942),

A sheltered spinster is brought out of her shell
By her psychiatrist" and "Steven Boyd, Jack Hawkins
In *The Third Secret* (1964), a psychoanalyst's

Daughter asks a patient to help her find her father's
Murderer." Like a cowboy, the only child roams
The lonely ranges and secret mesas of his genre.

XVII. *Their Patients*

As a rule, the patients I know do not pace
Furiously, nor scream, nor shoot doctors. For them,
To be a patient seems not altogether different

From one's interest in Ann Landers and her clients:
Her virtue of taking it all on, answering
Any question (artificial insemination by grandpa;

The barracuda of a girl who says that your glasses
Make you look square) and her virtue of saying,
Buster (or Dearie) stop complaining and do

What you want . . . and often that seems to be the point:
After the glassware from Design Research, after
A place on the Cape with Marimekko drapes,

The superlative radio and shoes, comes
The contingency tax—serious people, their capacity
For mere hedonism fills up, one seems to need

To perfect more complex ideas of desire,
To overcome altruism in the technical sense,
To learn to say no when you mean no and yes

When you mean yes, a standard of *cui bono*, a standard
Which, though it seems to be the inverse
Of more Spartan or Christian codes, is no less

Demanding in its call, inward in this case, to duty.
It suggests a kind of league of men and women dedicated
To their separate, inward duties, holding in common

Only the most general standard, or no standard
Other than valuing a sense of the conflict
Among standards, a league recalling in its mutual

Conflict and comfort the well-known fact that psychiatrists,
Too, are the patients of other psychiatrists,
Working dutifully—*cui bono*—at the inward standards.

XVIII. *The Mad*

Other patients are ill otherwise, and do
Scream and pace and kill or worse; and that
Should be recalled. Kit Smart, Hitler,

The contemporary poets of lunacy—none of them
Helps me to think of the mad otherwise
Than in clichés too broad, the maenads

And wild-eyed killers of the movies . . .
But perhaps lunacy feels something like a cliché,
A desperate or sweet yielding to some broad,

Mechanical simplification, a dispersal
Of the unbearable into its crude fragments,
The distraction of a repeated gesture

Or a compulsively hummed tune. Maybe
It is not utterly different from chewing
At one's fingernails. For the psychiatrists

It must come to seem ordinary, its causes
And the causes of its relief, after all,
No matter how remote and intricate, are no

Stranger than life itself, which was born or caused
Itself, once, as a kind of odor, a faint wreath
Brewing where the radiant light from billions

Of miles off strikes a faint broth from water
Standing in rock; life born from the egg
Of rock, and the egglike rock of death

Are no more strange than this other life
Which we name after the moon, lunatic
Other-life . . . housed, for the lucky ones,

In McLean Hospital with its elegant,
Prep-school atmosphere. When my friend
Went in, we both tried to joke: "Karen," I said,

"You must be crazy to spend money and time
In this place"—she gained weight,
Made a chess-board, had a roommate

Who introduced herself as the Virgin Mary,
Referred to another patient: "Well, she must
Be an interesting person, if she's in here."

XIX. Peroration, Defining Happiness

"I know not how it is, but certainly I
Have never been more tired with any reading
Than with dissertations upon happiness,

Which seems not only to elude inquiry,
But to cast unmerciful loads of clay
And sand and husks and stubble

Along the high-road of the inquirer.
Even sound writers talk mostly in a drawling
And dreaming way about it. He,

Who hath given the best definition
Of most things, hath given but an imperfect one,
Here, informing us that a happy life

Is one without impediment to virtue. . . .
In fact, hardly anything which we receive
For truth is really and entirely so,

Let it appear plain as it may, and let
Its appeal be not only to the understanding,
But to the senses; for our words do not follow

The senses exactly; and it is by words
We receive truth and express it."
So says Walter Savage Landor in his Imaginary

Conversation between Sir Philip Sidney
And Fulke Greville, Lord Brooke, all three,
In a sense, my own psychiatrists, shrinking

The sense of contingency and confusion
Itself to a few terms I can quote, ponder
Or type: the idea of wisdom, itself, shrinks.

XX. *Peroration, Concerning Genius*

As to my own concerns, it seems odd, given
The ideas many of us have about art,
That so many writers, makers of films,

Artists, all suitors of excellence and their own
Genius, should consult psychiatrists, willing
To risk that the doctor in curing

The sickness should smooth away the cicatrice
Of genius, too. But it is all bosh, the false
Link between genius and sickness,

Except perhaps as they were linked
By the Old Man, addressing his class
On the first day: "*I know why you are here.*

*You are here to laugh. You have heard of a crazy
Old man who believes that Robert Bridges
Was a good poet; who believes that Fulke*

*Greville was a great poet, greater than Philip
Sidney; who believes that Shakespeare's Sonnets
Are not all that they are cracked up to be. . . . Well,*

I will tell you something: I will tell you
What this course is about. Sometime in the middle
Of the Eighteenth Century, along with the rise

Of capitalism and scientific method, the logical
Foundations of Western thought decayed and fell apart.
When they fell apart, poets were left

With emotions and experiences, and with no way
To examine them. At this time, poets and men
Of genius began to go mad. Gray went mad. Collins

Went mad. Kit Smart was mad. William Blake surely
Was a madman. Coleridge was a drug addict, with severe
Depression. My friend Hart Crane died mad. My friend

Ezra Pound is mad. But you will not go mad; you will grow up
To become happy, sentimental old college professors,
Because they were men of genius, and you

Are not; and the ideas which were vital
To them are mere amusement to you. I will not
Go mad, because I have understood those ideas. . . ."

He drank wine and smoked his pipe more than he should;
In the end his doctors in order to prolong life
Were forced to cut away most of his tongue.

That was their business. As far as he was concerned
Suffering was life's penalty; wisdom armed one
Against madness; speech was temporary; poetry was truth.

XXI. Conclusion

Essaying to distinguish these men and women,
Who try to give medicine for misery,
From the rest of us, I find I have failed

To discover what essential statement could be made
About psychiatrists that would not apply
To all human beings, or what statement

About all human beings would not apply
Equally to psychiatrists. They, too,
Consult psychiatrists. They try tentatively

To understand, to find healing speech. They work
For truth and for money. They are contingent . . .
They talk and talk . . . they are, in the words

Of a lute-player I met once who despised them,
"Into machines" . . . all true of all, so that it seems
That "psychiatrist" is a synonym for "human being,"

Even in their prosperity which is perhaps
Like their contingency merely more vivid than that
Of lutanists, opticians, poets—all into

Truth, into music, into yearning, suffering,
Into elegant machines and luxuries, with caroling
And kisses, with soft rich cloth and polished

Substances, with cash, tennis and fine electronics,
Liberty of lush and reverend places—goods
And money in their contingency and spiritual

Grace evoke the way we are all psychiatrists,
All fumbling at so many millions of miles
Per minute and so many dollars per hour

Through the exploding or collapsing spaces
Between stars, saying what we can.

TRANSLATIONS

HOMECOMING

(Paul Celan)

Snowfall, thicker and thicker,
dovecolored, like yesterday,
snowfall, as if you were asleep just now.

Into the distance, the stacked-up whiteness
and beyond it, endless,
the sleigh-trace of the lost.

Below, hidden,
pushing itself upward,
the thing that hurts the eyes so much,
mound after mound,
unseeable.

On each mound,
hailed home to its own *today*,
sucked down into its muteness: an I
of wood, a post.

There: a feeling—
blown across by the icewind,
it fastens its dove-, its snow-
colored cloth bannerwise.

LOVE CROWN

(Paul Celan)

Now autumn nibbles its leaf from my hand: we are friends.
We take time out of a nutshell and teach it how to go:
time turns and goes back into its shell.

Now in the mirror it is Sunday,
in the dream there is a place for the calm of sleep,
in the mouth, the taste of truth.

My eye moves down the belly of my love:
we see one another,
we speak the darkness to ourselves,
we love one another like poppy and remembrance,
we sleep like the liquor in seashells,
like the ocean in the bloodbeams of the moon.

We stand at the window embracing, they see us from the street,
it is time they knew!
It is time that the stone let itself break into flower,
that the unresting have a heartbeat.
It is time there was time.

It is time.

BODY

(Boris Christov)

The spirit is in bed, it has been sleeping away
For hours now, but my body is awake and prowling
The dark streets like an owl intent on its prey,
Heedless of the roosters in the hills, already calling.

It stalks on into the dawn, peers into a drain
Or a murky ditch, trips over a shadow in its way,
Scrapes itself on a stone façade. Rivers of rain
Drum on my head, but can't wash the mud away.

My mouth, which has been silent such a long time
Holding its teeth clenched tight, now opens wide
And I imagine I hear the ocean of wine
That it has swallowed, sloshing around inside.

The blood pumps into the very nails of my toes,
It hits the heels and like an ape leaps up again.
A little ulcer flares like a torch that throws
Red light on the invisible jungle within.

The legs get back into action, the stiff joints crank
Gunpowder into their muscles to move them, the twist
Of the left knee pulling westward, the other shank
Dragging its faithful shoe towards the east.

The body quivers, it has decided to fly
Above the earth to the yellow throne of dawn . . .
But it can't take off with the violations that weigh
Heavily on its mudstained wings, holding them down.

Malicious with impotence—blind mouse forced to suck
At the stony tit of a nut—it has to slog
Heavily on through the rain. It writes on the sidewalk
The words *Live like a bird—die like a dog.*

SPIRIT

(Boris Christov)

While waiting for my body to stuff itself
Hunched over its dish of stewmeat and its glass,
My spirit flew away: a celestial wolf
Trotting the heavens on its invisible paws.

Where are you headed for through infinite space,
Proud flier, howling at the dark around you?
In the boundless universe, could there be any place
Still undiscovered, beyond these that surround you?

But from the moment that the spirit-wolf trod
Among the stars he was coursing toward the purlieus
Of the hidden sheepfold where the lambs of God
Graze the deep grasses of Paradise's meadows.

The gates, in ruin for many a millennium,
Lay in a heap close by a cherry tree.
With a predator's watchful air about him,
My spirit wriggled under the fence stealthily.

"Wait a minute, you winged wolf, before you dare
Sneak into that trap of knowledge. It will snap once,
Then nothing will be left of you in there.
You'll eat at yourself till nothing's left but bones."

But how can anything cross the mighty gulf
Of deafness that yawns between the lips and the ears?
Having strangled the Lamb of God, the wolf
Of my spirit padded the moon-path among the stars.

The ram who saw him in the dark began to weep.
The plaintive bleating of the whole flock joined his cry.
The cosmos itself burst into tears with the sheep,
And blood-stained stars fell from the grieving sky.

Meanwhile, on earth, my body was wiping the grease
From its muzzle. Drinking and eating too much made it heavy.
On the table before it, instead of the Golden Fleece,
Lay only a mess of bones in a puddle of gravy.

SONG ON PORCELAIN

(Czeslaw Milosz, after World War II)

Rose colored cup and saucer,
Flowery demitasses:
They lie beside the river
Where an armored column passes.
Winds from across the meadow
Sprinkle the banks with down;
A torn apple tree's shadow
Falls on the muddy path;
The ground everywhere is strewn
With bits of brittle froth—
Of all things broken and lost
The porcelain troubles me most.

Before the first red tones
Begin to warm the sky
The earth wakes up, and moans.
It is the small sad cry
Of cups and saucers cracking,
The masters' precious dream
Of roses, of mowers raking
And shepherds on the lawn.
The black underground stream
Swallows the frozen swan.
This morning, as I walked past
The porcelain troubled me most.

The blackened plain spreads out
To where the horizon blurs
In a litter of handle and spout,
A lively pulp that stirs
And crunches under my feet.
Pretty, useless foam:
Your stained colors are sweet—
Some bloodstained, in dirty waves

Flecking the fresh black loam
In the mounds of these new graves.
In sorrow and pain and cost
The porcelain troubles me most.

ISAAC LEYBUSH PERETZ

(Moshe Leib Halpern)

And so you're dead. And you're not underground yet,
And all over the world, hustlers of all ages
Rush out into the street like galloping horses
To sell the papers that print the headlines
That arrive with all the speed of the telegraph
To scream the news: your heart's not beating anymore.
And just like a splashy full-page advertisement
Here is your gray head framed in black. And we,
We big-shots who should be stricken dumb and prostrate,
Gather in a circle around your spirit
Like bar-girls clustered around a rich old drunk.
And we have tears, and words like smooth round pearls,
Like big gold coins. And everybody who has a tongue
Is beating out a dirge like a shoemaker's helper
Banging a thick nail through an old shoe's heel.
And in every stroke you can hear the dirt and the sweat
Dark, like Negro flesh. And everything is merchandise—
To Hell with it, to the Black Year with it,
We'll handle anything that can be bought and sold:
Torahs and pig's bristles, men and devil's dirt.
It's a wonder that we haven't cheated Death
Out of his artist's tools with coppers and schnapps.
We are the flesh and blood of that great hero Jacob,
Who bought his birthright cheap for a pot of beans,
You might say. And one of us, a full-fledged god,
You might say, made a deal for the entire world
For thirty silver shekels. So you might say.
And if that's all true, dear spirit, why shouldn't we deal
In you today? You, dust of our pride, what were you for us?
A last charred log still burning in a gypsy camp.
The sail of a ship wrestling a storm at night.
The last tree living in a tangled, bewitched forest
Where lightning destroyed thousand-year-old oaks,
Dead to the root. And now, what are you now?
A man on the cold ground, meaninglessly mute, a piece

Of marble whittled at by deathlight. An alphaomega.
An image—a moment's vision of the long sleep
That comes to take away our day and our night,
The little bit of life we like so much, containing
All the world's beauty. And is this our peace?
The hope of our dark way?
Why does a man bow down before the death thought?
Why does he snuffle like a child alone in the dark?
Who's in charge of the world? Who tells the springtime
To come and blossom, and to go away, and hurls the wind
Howling through the woods and over the fields, in the fall?

And when an eagle dies—why does the raven have to come
To peck out both its eyes?
Why do hands have to reach out and touch
The dead lion, without fear? Isn't the lion's soul
Supposed to roar from the flayed hide,
The kingly soul surviving the rotten corpse?
Excuse me—forgive me for asking, I'm sorry,
But what can I do, I also love my life,
Look, I've got eyes, and they're open.
And I am blind. I'm sorry—I'm only
A low-class ma-and-pa grocer's kid, I thirsted
Like dry earth panting for rain, to get
Some kind of vision from you, and even now
The thought of your spirit gone still makes me
Hungry: a beggar trembling at the sight of bread.
I want to see your soul: it has turned away.
And I see only night in you and death in you
And desolation, emptier for me than ever.
And blessed is he who believes in the world to come,
He has his comfort—For me, nothing:
A nothing that *is*.
For me, there's a yortzeit candle
Spending itself in smoke,
For me, there's a gravestone sinking into the earth,
And for me, there's the riddle of death to read
Over and over, with its little sickle
Glittering in front of me like some kind of fire—
A red fire, but somehow like something
Golden and something like blood.

THE RHYME OF REB NACHMAN

Reb Nachman sat in his hovel one day in spring
A hundred years ago. A linnet sang
Hidden in a flowering pear tree that reached a cloud
Of white to the window where his head was bowed
Uncovered over his book. His red hair glowed
In a mild shaft of sun as he read aloud—

Varoosh, dom, domyagel kashir.
Navroosh dom rishak, narfaz abir—

Seventeen syllables of the forbidden book
Of Kabal that the Kabalists call "The Black,"
The "Never-Uttered."
                        These and seven more
The young Reb spoke, and at his study door
He waited, cocking his copper head to listen,
Eager and fearful, for the steps of Satan—
And after a minute hearing and seeing nothing,
Angry and relieved, he cursed and said a blessing.

The peddler who sold him the book had sworn it was taken
By Gypsies out of the grave of the learned magician
Malmud of Cairo—Then let the Gypsies have it
To bury again! he thought, and went to move it
From the scarred reading table. Scrolls and stacked
Volumes half-hid the birchwood surface—cracked
With hairlines, worn cloudy-smooth by the sleeves and eyes
Of a thousand scholars groping through the maze
Of commentaries.
                        Then the Reb gasped: the grain,
Like an ancient text restored, was alive again—
Up through the layers of varnish, the wood had sprouted
Seven fresh sprigs of pale green birch!
                                          He shouted,

And feeling the shock run through him as a chill
He glanced outside. On the open window's sill
A blasted litter of petals, the color of dust,
Stirred in the mild air—as if a sudden frost
Had stricken it the pear-tree branch was denuded,
And brittle-black, the tree itself still crowded
With heavy blossoms where the linnet fluted
Prettily as before.
                              "Now Death-in-Life is mated,"
The scholar said, "with Life-in-Death—and Learning,
Child of Creation, has sent Creation turning
Against herself.
                              Varoosh, dom, domyagel kashir.
Navroosh dom rishak, narfaz abir—"
                                                  and here
The cultured voice of another finished the spell.

He turned, and saw a figure not from Hell
But from the earth, with earth and earthy creatures
Clinging to his bloodless skin. Among the fissures
And flaps of flesh, Reb Nachman could make out
The bone and binding gristle.
                              The other sat
In Nachman's chair, and spoke:
                                                  "I am Malmud,
Envoy of the One you seek. What earthly good
Or evil you desire from the Lord of Craving,
Speak it now—riches beyond all limit, the having
Of women or boys, gluttonies of Rome or potions
Of languid Egypt, the rites of Set or sensations
Of Pan—or perhaps for those you envy, evil:
Ecstasies of pain and humiliation, some rival
Scholar to be pocked with boils, his children hurt
And his wife prostituted: while to your court
He scorching himself with envy watches a stream
Of sages and the haughtiest *Rabbinim*
Make humble pilgrimage to glean the crumbs
Of cast-off wisdom at your feet, which comes
To them as manna—while the major feast
You save for private conference with the best:
The most feared kings, great artists, the more than rich,
The worshipped beauties, all of whom you teach

While all pay gifts and tribute, all in their kind
Competing to share that treasure of your mind!"

The corpse's voice grew louder, as if excited
By the motions of its own dead heart. It waited,
A pale worm feeding on its brow, to hear
The young Reb's answer.
                              Joy drowned Nachman's fear
Consciously. Coolly he watched the festering skin
Mobile around the mouth, and coolly took in
The speech of Malmud, eager to answer. He spoke:

"Childishness! Banal daydreams! You mistake
Nachman of Brendau for some half-learned child
Eager to fall, or a senile sexton, beguiled
By schnapps to memories of the passionate youth
He never had. I, Nachman, seek the truth
For my own causes, to write with my own hand
The secret knowledge I myself command
And make obedient, not to a crowd's applause,
As you conjurors do, but to my soul's own laws.
I have not outstripped the mystics and professors
Of Lvov and Brendau merely to gain the pleasures
Of drunken peasants, or students on a spree—

To know, to know, to know, to hear and see.
It is Knowledge I require—and trade my soul
To finish it, like a book—but Knowledge whole:
Not partial lust, revenge, joy, horror, the toys
That bait the common soul—
                              yes, those, but those
Entirely: all that the human mind and passion
Have ever endured, compacted in one night's vision
As in the letters KASHIR Kabalah has fused
All darkness."
              "Is that all?" asked the corpse, amused.

"No," said the scholar, "More, I want to see
The future of the world that is to be
For a hundred years. Then, having in the span
Of one night known a thousand lives of man
(As I know Satan can let me do), to make

2 9 4

That knowledge, having lived it, into a book:
Then, when in mind and on paper I have possessed
So much of life, let your Master have the rest."

"So be it," said Malmud.
                              A maggot crept
From his eye's corner, as if he winked or wept.

"Baal," he recited, "Baal-z-Baob, Thou colder
Than cold, whose member spits out snow, while sulphur
And phosphorus fire Thy heart—drink up this soul,
And let it drink the world. Send Nachman from Sheol
New organs of increase, male and female, to grow
By dozens on his body, that he may know
All pleasures, like thy child Tiresias. Seed
His eyes and brain with visions till they bleed.
Show him the interstices of the soul
In prolonged exquisite detail, to taste it all
Corpuscle by corpuscle—like that subtle Persian
Who starved his captive rival and had the surgeon
(Afterwards tenderly dressing the incision)
Cut off a little flesh each day, for the kitchen
To seethe in tempting sauces which the gentiles
Devise for unclean meat, with savory smells
To make the caitiff starving in his cell
Knowingly devour himself.
                              Lastly, from Hell,
Convey from Thy ovens images of flame
To paint him knowledge of the times to come—
Wars, arts, plagues, devices, passions, inventions,
Assemblies, tortures, adulteries, interrogations,
Trials and spectacles—
                              and let him take
His knowledge to him and have it in his book."

And then, "Varoosh, dom, domyagel kashir,"
He chanted, "Navroosh dom rishak, narfaz abir—"
And finished the spell.
                              All that afternoon
The linnet sang to the milky daylight moon.
Bees dove and rose among the pear-tree flowers
Until the sun sank low. All through the hours

Of the mild evening and the springtime night a voice,
Low and unyielding, murmured in the little house.
No lamp was lit, but through the darkest hours
The tireless voice persisted, while the powers
Of Hell in visions and dictation unrolled
The Scroll of Time for Nachman.
                         When the bird called
Questioning with the waking sun, the house was still,
Save for the petals that whispered on the sill—
And stayed so all day, till the Sabbath Eve drew near
And Nachman's brethren in study tried his door.

They found the corpse of Malmud in the chair,
Inanimate, the cold mouth pulled in a sneer,
And on the couch that faced him, another thing:
Man-sized and shaped, that rustling and trembling
Moved in the breeze—an effigy, it seemed,
That Nachman in his forbidden arts had framed
Of paper and parchment from old texts.
                            Dry paper
Were the lips and eyes, and paper the color of copper
Shredded and tarnished the twisted hair and beard,
Crumbling and printed with letters. While they stared
It moved as if alive. One arm of flaking
And dense-packed paper, heavily, as if seeking
A closer audience with them, lifted and gestured
As the dry mouth rustled.
                      "I have read the Law," it whispered,
"In company with its Author, that you call God.
Sitting at His side, I have interpreted
The prophets who wrote Him onto the Scroll of Time,
Where He wrote them in turn, in rhymeless rhyme.
I have seen the nations broken in His hand.
We came to him as a Word, or less—a sound
That led to a dozen more, the way a child
Makes up a song. Your rituals are reviled
In heaven, and your studies—"
                          Here the shape
As if exhausted fell back in a fluttering heap
Smelling of old books.
                    None had dared come near
While the man of paper whispered, but they could hear
The mouth shape noises now like leaves on a midden

Shuffled by the wind, and recognized the Forbidden
Epitome:
> Varoosh, dom, domyagel kashir.
> Navroosh dom rishak, narfaz abir
> Shattan mah kafirzi—
>> and one syllable more,
Best not pronounced.
>> The Rabbins prayed at the door,
Nailed shut with nails of lead, for eleven days
Without remission, and performed the obsequies
For Nachman under the pear tree: afraid to touch
The body, if body it was, that lay on the couch,
Or the unclean remains of that magician
Malmud of Cairo.
>> At last in solemn convention
The Rabbinic Councils of Brendau and Lvov
Discussed the case, and in their edict gave
Instructions: that the hovel and all it contained
Be burned to finest ashes, as might be strained
Through Sabbath cheesecloth; and that they bury the ashes,
With holy prayers for the dead, in the Pripet Marshes.

FROM *THE INFERNO OF DANTE*: CANTO XXXIV

"And now, *Vexilla regis prodeunt*
   Inferni—therefore, look," my master said
   As we continued on the long descent,

"And see if you can make him out, ahead."
   As though, in the exhalation of heavy mist
   Or while night darkened our hemisphere, one spied

A mill—blades turning in the wind, half-lost
   Off in the distance—some structure of that kind
   I seemed to make out now. But at a gust

Of wind, there being no other shelter at hand,
   I drew behind my leader's back again.
   By now (and putting it in verse I find

Fear in myself still) I had journeyed down
   To where the shades were covered wholly by ice,
   Showing like straw in glass—some lying prone,

And some erect, some with the head toward us,
   And others with the bottoms of the feet;
   Another like a bow, bent feet to face.

When we had traveled forward to the spot
   From which it pleased my master to have me see
   That creature whose beauty once had been so great,

He made me stop, and moved from in front of me.
   "Look: here is Dis," he said, "and here is the place
   Where you must arm yourself with the quality

Of fortitude." How chilled and faint I was
   On hearing that, you must not ask me, reader—
   I do not write it; words would not suffice:

I neither died, nor kept alive—consider
  With your own wits what I, alike denuded
  Of death and life, became as I heard my leader.

The emperor of the realm of grief protruded
  From mid-breast up above the surrounding ice.
  A giant's height, and mine, would have provided

Closer comparison than would the size
  Of his arm and a giant. Envision the whole
  That is proportionate to parts like these.

If he was truly once as beautiful
  As he is ugly now, and raised his brows
  Against his Maker—then all sorrow may well

Come out of him. How great a marvel it was
  For me to see three faces on his head:
  In front there was a red one; joined to this,

Each over the midpoint of a shoulder, he had
  Two others—all three joining at the crown.
  That on the right appeared to be a shade

Of whitish yellow; the third had such a mien
  As those who come from where the Nile descends.
  Two wings spread forth from under each face's chin,

Strong, and befitting such a bird, immense—
  I have never seen at sea so broad a sail—
  Unfeathered, batlike, and issuing three winds

That went forth as he beat them, to freeze the whole
  Realm of Cocytus that surrounded him.
  He wept with all six eyes, and the tears fell

Over his three chins mingled with bloody foam.
  The teeth of each mouth held a sinner, kept
  As by a flax-rake: thus he held three of them

In agony. For the one the front mouth gripped,
  The teeth were as nothing to the claws, which sliced
  And tore the skin until his back was stripped.

"That soul," my master said, "who suffers most,
    Is Judas Iscariot; head locked inside,
    He flails his legs. Of the other two, who twist

With their heads down, the black mouth holds the shade
    Of Brutus; writhing, but not a word will he scream;
    Cassius is the sinewy one on the other side.

But night is rising again, and it is time
    That we depart, for we have seen the whole."
    As he requested, I put my arms round him,

And waiting until the wings were opened full
    He took advantage of the time and place
    And grasped the shaggy flank, and gripping still,

From tuft to tuft descended through the mass
    Of matted hair and crusts of ice. And then,
    When we had reached the pivot of the thighs,

Just where the haunch is at its thickest, with strain
    And effort my master brought around his head
    To where he'd had his legs: and from there on

He grappled the hair as someone climbing would—
    So I supposed we were heading back to Hell.
    "Cling tight, for it is stairs like these," he sighed

Like one who is exhausted, "which we must scale
    To part from so much evil." Then he came up
    Through a split stone, and placed me on its sill,

And climbed up toward me with his cautious step.
    I raised my eyes, expecting I would see
    Lucifer as I left him—and saw his shape

Inverted, with his legs held upward. May they
    Who are too dull to see what point I had passed
    Judge whether it perplexed me. "Come—the way

Is long, the road remaining to be crossed
    Is hard: rise to your feet," the master said,
    "The sun is at mid-tierce." We had come to rest

In nothing like a palace hall; instead
  A kind of natural dungeon enveloped us,
  With barely any light, the floor ill-made.

"Before I free myself from the abyss,
  My master," I said when I was on my feet,
  "Speak, and dispel my error: where is the ice?

And how can he be fixed head-down like that?
  And in so short a time, how can it be
  Possible for the sun to make its transit

From evening to morning?" He answered me,
  "You imagine you are still on the other side,
  Across the center of the earth, where I

Grappled the hair on the evil serpent's hide
  Who pierces the world. And all through my descent,
  You were on that side; when I turned my head

And legs about, you passed the central point
  To which is drawn, from every side, all weight.
  Now you are on the opposite continent

Beneath the opposite hemisphere to that
  Which canopies the great dry land therein:
  Under the zenith of that one is the site

Whereon the Man was slain who without sin
  Was born and lived; your feet this minute press
  Upon a little sphere whose rounded skin

Forms the Judecca's other, outward face.
  Here it is morning when it is evening there;
  The one whose hair was like a ladder for us

Is still positioned as he was before.
  On this side he fell down from Heaven; the earth,
  Which till then stood out here, impelled by fear

Veiled itself in the sea and issued forth
  In our own hemisphere. And possibly,
  What now appears on this side fled its berth

And rushing upwards left a cavity:
   This hollow where we stand." There is below,
   As far from Beelzebub as one can be

Within his tomb, a place one cannot know
   By sight, but by the sound a little runnel
   Makes as it wends the hollow rock its flow

Has worn, descending through its winding channel:
   To get back up to the shining world from there
   My guide and I went into that hidden tunnel;

And following its path, we took no care
   To rest, but climbed: he first, then I—so far,
   Through a round aperture I saw appear

Some of the beautiful things that Heaven bears,
Where we came forth, and once more saw the stars.

NOTES
INDEX OF TITLES

NOTES

POEM WITH REFRAINS. The italicized lines are quotations from, in order: Thomas
Campion, Fulke Greville, Greville again, George Peele, Algernon Swinburne, and
Greville again.

THE DAY DREAMERS. The italicized lines are (deliberately) misquoted from the opening
lines of Walter Savage Landor's poem "Separation": "There is a mountain and a
wood between us, / Where the lone shepherd and late bird have seen us / Morning
and noon and even-tide repass."

AVENUE. Commentary written for *Best Poems of 1992*, edited by Charles Simic:

"Ideas get into our heads and we pursue them, sometimes for years or forever.
Long ago, possibly influenced by Pound's definition of the epic as a poem containing
history, I proposed to myself that poetry must imagine a community. That the
emphasis needed to be on 'imagine' I could tell from reading my first hero in the
art, Yeats. (What if I had attached myself to Stevens, instead?)

"So my poem 'Avenue' is one foray in a lifelong quest among the pronouns, *they,
I, we, he, she* and underneath them their provisional or arbitrary quality. Shall we
tell it to you in the first person? Would you tell it to them in the third person?
Might I try it in the second person? And so forth.

"The poem also has roots in the High Holy Days as I experienced them as a
child—the hypnotic appeal in fasting; the boredom and sudden emotion of the
prayers; pitching horse-chestnuts against the back wall of the synagogue; people in
stylish or frumpy dress-up clothes; the foreign otherworldly sensuousness of cantorial
singing; the climactic yet anti-climactic groan of the ram's horn; my grandparents
on one side watching Perry Como sing the *kol nidre* on television; my grandfather
on the other side avoiding the whole scene of devotion; the secular and Christian
world with its bright seductive October weather, its downtown, its Atlantic Ocean,
radiating and pulling on all sides away from the synagogue at the center.

"Though little of that material figures directly in the poem, 'Avenue' is concerned
with the peculiar English name of the Day of Atonement. 'Atonement,' which looks
like some Latin borrowing, is made out of the idea of being 'at one' with one's god,
or community, or vows, or even a person. Yom Kippur is the day of at-one-ment,
which chimes interestingly for me with the Christian and pagan holiday of the same
time of year: All Saints or All Spirits. All, one: a play of unity and diversity that in
turn makes me think of the fragmented, plural American city held together visibly
by words, by the signs and spoken or sung syllables of its streets, where all our 'they'
is also somehow 'one.'

"One fall, driving along the Finchley Road in London I saw in my headlights a
man lying in the roadway. He was passed-out drunk. I carried him into the entryway
of a shoe store, an incident I tell here from his point of view, in the first person,
as *I*, as one of all."

DESECRATION OF THE GRAVESTONE OF ROSE P. (1897–1924). My father's mother, Rose Schacter Pinsky, died in childbirth at the age of twenty-seven. Her photograph, preserved on metal under a dome of glass on her headstone, which is carved in the shape of a tree with truncated limbs, was partially destroyed when the Jewish cemetery in Long Branch, New Jersey, was vandalized. The poem mixes the unknown perpetrator's consciousness with Herbert's lines.

IF YOU COULD WRITE ONE GREAT POEM, WHAT WOULD YOU WANT IT TO BE ABOUT? The poem reports pretty faithfully the actual responses of four high school students. The young woman who answered "Sign" is partially blind as well as hearing-impaired.

INCANTATION. This is a translation based on Czeslaw Milosz's literal trot. There is an illuminating passage on the poem in Seamus Heaney's *The Government of the Tongue*.

THE WANT BONE

FROM THE CHILDHOOD OF JESUS. Based on two or three different stories in the Christian Apocrypha, where the child Jesus is frequently portrayed as unruly and destructive.

THE WANT BONE. In David Lehman's book *Ecstatic Occasions, Expedient Forms*, the editor invited poets to comment on form and creativity in one of their poems. Paragraphs contributed on "The Want Bone":

"Form in itself, like 'creativity' in itself, is cheap—it is already there, the starting place. All day long form keeps droning that x=x, every fulfilled expectation makes a form. And creating all day long the mind chatters like a sewing machine, stitching up its unlikely creatures. A billion per minute.

"It is the exception that exhilarates and inspires.

"The resistance to form gives form weight and passion, and attentive resistance to the endless mental stream of creation gives the mind shape and action. In this sense, all successful rhyme is slant rhyme: as with metaphor, it is the *un*likeness that delights and illuminates.

"The groan of wanting—the plainest English word for desire means not-having —was a physical sound and shape for me, and the form fell out as a procession of almost-having, the rhymes less than full, and rising at the ends of the unfulfilled odd-numbered lines *a* and *c* rather than the even closure of *b* and *d*, the pentameter sprung and oblate rather than fully rounded, the sound and shape of O never repeated to the full rhetorical possibility ('O my fin O my food O my flower my O my O,' etc.); all almost filled out or filled in, but not.

"This is retrospective, of course; at the time, there was the emotion, the O, and maybe a half-formed idea of something nearly florid and juicy, but scorched and spiny instead."

SHIVA AND PARVATI HIDING IN THE RAIN. The title comes from a miniature in the Museum of Fine Arts, Boston.

PICTURE. Based on the death of Lon Chaney.

PILGRIMAGE. Commentary for *Best Poems of 1990*, edited by Jorie Graham:

"The virtually sexual intensity of language and feeling in Psalm 139—the Hebrew poet's attempt to approach the absolute—inspired some of the phrases and setting in 'Pilgrimage.' I'll try to say a little not about the poem's meaning, but about the thinking and feeling behind it.

"The poem tries to imagine something like the early days of Judaism in a setting something like the Yosemite Falls of California. A paradigm, but with specific textures. The goal is less a conception of worship—far less any specific mode of worship—than a conception of passion in a place among a people. The ritual conceives an Absolute, but exactly because it is *conceived*, the Absolute is always changing and flowing like the falls or a sentence in a poem, something is always next or behind. Always near the peak, always on the way to it, always not at it."

Religion concerns me in *The Want Bone* not quite exactly in itself but as a vivid, charged example of the passion to create. Making rituals, making buildings, making names, making chants of like sounds, making music—all, in this context, make up the communal expression of what is sometimes called making love. Arousal flies up above a consciousness that this ardent making, in its deadly struggle with the imperfection of what was, may also twist into a passionate destroying: pogroms, extermination of American Indian civilizations, etc.

VOYAGE TO THE MOON. The names La Hire, Raquel, Argine, etc., are traditional Gypsy lore, as is the term "Suicide King" for the King of Hearts, based on the way he holds his sword. The sculptor and her works are fictional.

SHIRT. The story of the man who assists the women, then leaps himself, appears in newspaper accounts of the Triangle Shirtwaist fire, but the eyewitness has not been identified. The story may or may not be myth.

AT PLEASURE BAY. Pleasure Bay is a real place, part of my home town of Long Branch, New Jersey, where the Shrewsbury River meets the Atlantic Ocean. My father has often pointed out to me where the chief of police and his lover committed suicide in a car.

HISTORY OF MY HEART

THE VOLUME. John Singleton Copley's painting *Brook Watson and the Shark* depicts what looks like a corpse being defended from a shark by sailors. (Contrary to the poem, Watson survived despite losing a leg to the shark, and commissioned the picture.)

THE NEW SADDHUS. I understand a Saddhu to be a wandering holy man, one who has renounced the world, a course taken in some cultures by males who reach a certain age.

SONG OF REASONS. The Dukes of Levis-Mirepoix and their remarkable claims regarding their ancestry are actual.

AN EXPLANATION OF AMERICA

LOCAL POLITICS. "The Eagle Stirreth Her Nest" is a powerful sermon, once available on LP, by the Reverend C. L. Franklin.

A LOVE OF DEATH. Much of the prairie material, including the incident of the stranger who leaps into the thresher, is paraphrased from *My Antonía*, by Willa Cather.

BRAVERIES. The story of the infant born in the middle of the Battle of Saguntum appears at the beginning of Ben Jonson's poem "To the Immortall Memorie, and Friendship of that Noble Pair, Sir Lucius Cary, and Sir H. Morison."

SADNESS AND HAPPINESS

DISCRETIONS OF ALCIBIADES. My idea of the flamboyant figure Alcibiades comes from Plutarch's account.

LIBRARY SCENE. My friend, a scholar, turned forty on the occasion of Richard Nixon's greatest electoral triumph, and the next day had to address an audience of donors to Wellesley College, many of them politically conservative.

ESSAY ON PSYCHIATRISTS. The "Old Man" of section XX is based, but not exactly, on Yvor Winters.

TRANSLATIONS

The translations from Boris Christov are based on English versions provided by William Meredith and Richard Harteisz for their anthology *Window in the Black Sea: Poetry from Bulgaria* (Carnegie Mellon, 1992).

The translation from Czeslaw Milosz is based on an English version provided by Czeslaw Milosz.

THE RHYME OF REB NACHMAN. This poem, first written for the annual Halloween Reading at the Blacksmith House in Cambridge, was attributed to a fictional author. It is a kind of translation with no original.

INDEX OF TITLES